D0975782

Managing the Unexpected

Managing the Unexpected

Sustained Performance in a Complex World

Third Edition

Karl E. Weick
Kathleen M. Sutcliffe

WILEY

For general information about our other products and services, please contact our Customer Care Department within the United States at (800) 762-2974, outside the United States at (317) 572-3993 or fax (317) 572-4002.

Wiley publishes in a variety of print and electronic formats and by print-on-demand. Some material included with standard print versions of this book may not be included in e-books or in print-on-demand. If this book refers to media such as a CD or DVD that is not included in the version you purchased, you may download this material at http://booksupport.wiley.com. For more information about Wiley products, visit www.wiley.com.

ISBN 978-1-118-86241-4 (cloth); ISBN 978-1-118-86245-2 (ePDF); ISBN 978-1-118-86249-0 (ePub)

Printed in the United States of America

10 9 8 7 6 5

Contents

Preface

U nexpected events can be disorganizing. It takes both anticipation and resilience to manage unexpected disruptions, a
combination that we call *mindful organizing*. This pattern was
implicit in the original studies of high reliability organizations
(HROs) and became more explicit as a more varied set of
organizations were examined. These increases in variety, however, did not always deepen our understanding of the basic
processes involved. That judgment is less a criticism than it is
the identification of a niche.

In the two previous editions of this book, we also have
discussed processes of high reliability that could be adopted
more widely. In this third edition we are more concerned with
foundations. We still add to variety by exploring elements of high
reliability organizing in settings such as banking, museum curating, latent fingerprint identification, aircraft piloting, and automobile manufacturing. But we spend more time discussing the
complexity of each of the five principles that are built on failure,
simplification, operations, resilience, and expertise. Our intent is
to show that considerable collective commitment and competence
are necessary, both to deploy these five in the face of the
unexpected and to organize around them in order to sustain
performance. Managing the unexpected is not simply an exercise
in going down a checklist. Indeed, one of the ironies of probing
deeper into the complexities of high reliability organizing is that

the principles gain new relevance for everyday life lived in places that are not large, high-hazard, technical systems. We argue that microlevel and mesolevel patterns impose constraints on more macro systems. Thus, one way to approach this book is to treat it as an analysis of the experience of reliability. Crucial moments in that experience occur when people size up and act on the unexpected before it escalates out of control. Those moments are crucial because nonobvious disruptions can be handled in two different ways. They can be normalized away as familiar or made to stand out when they are anomalized as unfamiliar. Resolving the disruption one way or the other depends on how people organize their activities. This line of argument introduces a sense of agency rather than fatalism into settings that often appear monolithic, closed, and rigid. Our inspiration clearly remains HROs. Our aim is to dig deeper into the human side of what works for them.

This third edition differs from previous editions in several ways. We pay more attention to sensemaking, interacting, and language, mindful of wildland firefighter David Allen's comment, "You presume that people in HROs are already communicating." He's right. We did presume that and now try to give that presumption more substance. We analyze a broader range of cases in an effort to show the generalizability of mindful organizing directed at sustained reliable performance. We devote a full chapter to each of the five principles to illustrate the context that supports them, complications that they entail, and ways they can be woven into current functioning in most organizations. The relationship of our argument to topics such as organizational safety and risk management is one of a shared concern with order and recurring action patterns. In our case, we try to describe the performative character of order creation and maintenance and the agency that this implies. Organizing holds events together and reliable performance depends on sustained organizing. But the organizing that we discuss should not be confused with organizational design. In many ways, organizing as we discuss it amounts to workarounds necessitated by flawed formal designs. Our frequent use of quotations from other sources is intentional. This style clarifies the lineage of ideas, anchors interpretations, and provides raw materials so that readers can make their own interpretations and customization.

Newer analyses of the original three HROs—an aircraft carrier, an air traffic control facility, and an electrical power generation unit—clarify that all three were "best of their class."[1] Our orientation is both to dig deeper into why they were best and, more important, to describe how groups not included in this class can get better.

Acknowledgments

Since publishing the second edition, we have continued to examine themes of reliability in organizing and have been greatly helped by people whose efforts we deeply appreciate. This revised third edition was strengthened by ongoing discussions with Daved van Stralen, Gary Provansal, Dan Kleinman, Michele Barton, Marlys Christianson, Kyle Weick, Tim Vogus, Dan Gruber, Paul Schulman, Tom Mercer, Maria Farkas, Erik Helzer, Sharon Kim, Peter Pronovost, Bob Wears, Dave Thomas, Bert Slagmolen, Annette Gerbauer, Randy Cadieux, Ralph Soule, Marc Flitter, Dionysiou Dionysis, and Barbara Czarniawska.

Our families have been lovingly patient with our efforts, and none of this would have been possible without them being there for us. Karen Weick and Tim Wintermute have held things together for all of us. To dedicate this book to them is an unduly small gesture, considering how much they mean to us.

1

Mismanaging the Unexpected

"A breakdown is not a negative situation to be avoided, but a situation of nonobviousness."[1]

—Terry Winograd and Fernando Flores

"Danger, disquiet, anxiety attend the unknown—the first instinct is to eliminate those distressing states. First principle: any explanation is better than none. . . . The first idea which explains that the unknown is in fact the known does so much good that one 'holds it for true.'"[2]

—Friedrich Nietzsche

Nonobvious breakdowns happen all the time. Some are a big deal. Most are not. But which are which? The answer to that question is hazy because we tend to settle for the "first explanation" that makes us feel in control. That explanation turns the

1

unknown into the known, which makes the explanation appear to be "true." That can be a serious misjudgment. This book is about what we could call "the second explanation," the one that—discomforting though it may be—treats the unknown *as knowable*. This second explanation is built from processes that produce an ongoing focus on failures, simplifications, operations, options, and expertise. Organizing that incorporates processes with these five areas of focus helps make breakdowns more knowable. These processes are an effortful means to maintain reliable performance, but previous work on high reliability organizations (HROs) shows that effortful processes like these make breakdowns more obvious at earlier stages in their development.

Our ideas come from an evolving body of work that originated with studies of safe operations on the flight decks of aircraft carriers, the generation and transmission of electrical power, and the dispatching of aircraft at an en route air traffic control center.[3] The common problem faced by all three was a million accidents waiting to happen *that didn't*. In each case the question was, How were the units organized to accomplish this outcome? Among the answers that have been proposed are the existence of a unique culture, capability for self-design, networks built on expertise, hybrid structures with special attention to redundancy, training and routines, situation awareness, mind-sets involved in sense-making, relational strategies, and information processing.[4] In an effort to synthesize a workable set of principles from this rich array, we focused on processes that were mixtures of variety and stability or, as the late Michael Cohen called them, "patterns in variety."[5] One *pattern* that seemed to recur was a sustained focus on small failures, less abstract specifics, ongoing operations, alternative pathways to keep going, and the mobilization of expertise. The *variety* within this pattern came from local customizing that produced meaningful practices that did not compromise the adaptive capacity that the pattern generated.

Once that adaptive capacity weakens, reliability suffers. To illustrate how problems with reliability develop over time, in this chapter we analyze the collapse of the Washington Mutual Bank (WaMu). Although this example involves the financial industry, the problems and lessons apply to other industries as well.[6] This wider application occurs because all of us, just as was true for those at WaMu, have to act in situations we can't possibly understand.[7] And the reason we can't understand them is because all of us "have to apply limited conceptions to unlimited interdependencies."[8] The conceptions and the ways we apply them are what matter. If we change these conceptions, then we change our ability to function under conditions of nonobviousness. As we will see, WaMu underestimated its interdependencies and overestimated its conceptual grasp of those interdependencies it did see.

Washington Mutual Mismanages the Unexpected

Washington Mutual Bank (WaMu) failed and was seized by the Federal Deposit Insurance Corporation (FDIC) on September 25, 2008, at 6 PM, and sold to JP Morgan Chase. We take a closer look at a sample of surprises in this unit that affected its reliability. And we describe one way to think about these fluctuations in reliability. Our interpretation is grounded in the idea that *managing* the unexpected is an ongoing effort to define and monitor weak signals[9] of potentially more serious threats and to take adaptive action as those signals begin to crystallize into more complex chains of unintended consequences. The phrase "begin to crystallize" is crucial to our argument because managing is an active process that is spread over time as the signals and situations change. As a problem begins to unfold, weak signals are hard to detect but easy to remedy. As time passes, this state of affairs tends to reverse. Signals become easy to detect but hard to remedy.

As weak signals change, so do the requirements for adaptive functioning. It is that adapting that became more and more flawed at WaMu.

Overview of Washington Mutual Bank Failure[10]

During the 1980s WaMu, nearly 100 years old, was a retail savings and loan (S&L) bank that, under chief executive officer (CEO) Louis Pepper, had grown from 35 branches to 50 and from $2 billion in assets to $7 billion. The organization was held together by five values, all nouns: ethics, respect, teamwork, innovation, and excellence.[11] When Pepper was replaced in December 1988 by Kerry Killinger, the values were changed to three adjectives: fair, caring, and human.[12] Later, as the bank aggressively tried to become the largest at several lines of business (largest S&L, largest mortgage lender,[13] and largest home equity lender[14]) and focused increasingly on high-risk, subprime loans, two new adjectives replaced all other values: dynamic and driven.[15] These last two values were christened "The WaMu way."[16]

In 1998 WaMu acquired Long Beach Mortgage (LB), a small subprime lender with $328 million in assets. Subprime lending had become fashionable in the banking industry. WaMu had never made these kinds of loans although they appeared to be more profitable than conventional mortgages, albeit riskier. Subprime loans were more profitable because banks charged higher interest rates and higher fees, but they were riskier because borrowers couldn't qualify for regular prime mortgages.

An early weak signal of unexpected events occurred in the summer of 2003. A sampling of 270 LB loans reviewed by the compliance department revealed that 40 percent were deemed "unacceptable because of a critical error."[17] Underwriting standards had been loosened to sell more loans. An internal flyer had said "a thin file is a good file,"[18] suggesting that less effort spent on documentation meant more time to sell more loans. For example, one loan application had a picture of a mariachi singer, and his income is "stated" as being in six figures. However, the picture was not a picture of the borrower, nor was that the borrower's income.[19]

As the bank moved into a higher risk strategy for residential loans, the chief risk officer, James Vanasek, faced the unenviable position of being "in charge of balancing risk, at a bank that was loading up on it."[20] Much later during a congressional hearing, Senator Tom Coburn asked Vanasek, "How do you account for the fact that somebody has seen a [housing] bubble, and by definition, a bubble is going to burst, and then their corporate strategy is to jump into the middle of the bubble?"[21] Vanasek had no answer then, nor did he have any success earlier when he tried to limit the number of "stated income" loans being made (loans with no proof of income). He resigned.

There was a continuing push to sell high-margin products, such as home equity loans and subprime loans. A new risk officer, Ron Cathcart, was hired as Vanasek's replacement, and soon thereafter, Cathcart told CEO Killinger that the Federal Office of Thrift Supervision (OTS) was about to downgrade the bank's "health" rating. Killinger said, "I don't like to hear bad news." Cathcart replied, "It's my job to deliver bad news," but Killinger was already out the door before Cathcart finished his sentence.[22]

During this period former CEO Pepper sent his protégé Killinger a blunt letter. The gist of it was that Killinger was not leading in the face of the bank's continuing decline.[23] For example, as Pepper put it, Killinger still held on to the title chief operating officer (COO) but operations were a mess. Even though Pepper said that it was imperative that Killinger hire a COO, Killinger didn't and kept the title.[24] Pepper was also deeply worried about Killinger's optimism and his failure to discuss worst-case scenarios. Pepper's worries were shared by insiders: "Don't listen to him, he's a Pollyanna."[25] As Pepper said in his letter, "There is no alternative but to give the worst case to the decision makers or later be in an untenable position of failing to make full disclosure. If you make full disclosure you may lose money but failure to do so has much worse penalties." No disclosure was made and much worse penalties did occur. As problems mounted the directors did next to nothing because they had little information about loans or borrowers. "When a borrower applied for a mortgage with limited documentation, no one kept track of which kind of documentation he or she had provided."[26]

In June 2006, in the face of an accelerating WaMu commitment to high-margin products, "something strange happened."[27] The median price of existing homes declined 1.7 percent year to year for the first time in 11 years, and home sales dropped a sudden 13 percent from the year before.[28] Other "strange" things happened. Borrowers started to miss mortgage payments but continued to make credit card payments (a reversal of normal priorities).[29] More loans were made with less documentation (insiders called them NINA loans: no income, no assets).[30] There were growing instances of first payment default (borrowers failed to make the first mortgage payment after the loan was granted).[31]

But why did all of this seem "strange"? What seemed to happen is that separate signals began to form a coherent, salient pattern. These patterns did not suddenly appear full-blown out of thin air. Instead, the clues had been emerging for some time.[32] But differences in employees' positions, as well as in their interests, power, competencies, incentives, and access to data, produced different levels of concern throughout the organization. Interpretations differed as well. We turn to five principles for managing the unexpected that were not followed at WaMu and could well have mitigated some of its problems.

Problems in Mindful Organizing at WaMu

In this book we focus on five hallmarks of organizations that perform remarkably well day after day under trying conditions and persistently have fewer than their fair share of crises. These hallmarks make up what we have termed *mindful organizing*. In this section we preview each of the five principles individually, provide examples of their relevance to WaMu's growing problems, and comment briefly on issues that will be developed more fully in subsequent chapters. Our intention is to illustrate the kinds of cues that stand out when we pay closer attention to indications of failure, simplification, operations, resilience, and expertise (FSORE).[33]

Preoccupation with Failure   The principle of a preoccupation with failure directs attention to ways in which your local activities can conceal or highlight such things as symptoms of system malfunction, small errors that could enlarge and spread, opportunities to speak up and be listened to, a gradual drift toward complacency, the need to pinpoint mistakes you don't want to make, and respect for your own day-to-day experience with surprises.

There were visible signs of failing at WaMu. For example, there were indications that guidelines for underwriting were being violated. Suspicions of fraud were investigated in Downey, California, where it was found that "red flags were overlooked, process requirements were waived, and exceptions to policy were granted."[34] People were working right up to an increasingly blurry edge that separated right from wrong. In sociologist Don Palmer's words,[35] wrongdoing had become normal although this was not always evident to the people who had been drawn in.

WaMu was aware of mistakes it didn't want to make (e.g., "We don't want their homes back"),[36] but it issued an underwhelming directive stating that employees "should be friendlier when they tried to collect overdue payments." All along there were signs that mistakes were being made that WaMu didn't want to make. There were signs of the growing possibility that borrowers would owe more on their houses than those houses were worth (they would be underwater). Speculation on single-family homes was also going up in the form of non–owner-occupied loans. Such loans are risky because borrowers would dump the home at the first sign of trouble. True, the borrower would lose money, but as the saying goes, "Your first loss is the best loss when you are in danger."[37] You minimize throwing good money after bad if you get out when the damage is small. Internally at WaMu, there was growing pressure to package and sell delinquency-prone loans to investors before the market detected that they had "soured."[38] By June 2007 bad loans had jumped 45 percent. $1.7 billion worth of loans were delinquent, and $750 million more were involved in mortgages that were being foreclosed.[39]

Perhaps the WaMu group most likely to be preoccupied with failure, whether it wants to or not, is the office of investor relations. Staff in this office have to "say bad things in good ways."[40] Investor anger funneled through their phones. As WaMu became more and more mismanaged, the anger voiced in calls to investor relations went up.[41] Mere frustrations, a weaker signal of trouble, gave way to rants, a much stronger signal of trouble. But the rants arrived too late to improve reliability.

Reluctance to Simplify   Another way HROs manage the unexpected is by being reluctant to accept simplifications. It is certainly true that success in any coordinated activity requires that people simplify to stay focused on a handful of key issues and indicators. But it is also true that less simplification allows you to see in more detail what might be causing the unexpected. HROs take deliberate steps to create more complete and nuanced pictures of what they face and who they are as they face it.

A costly simplification at WaMu occurred when managers treated all borrowers as similar and failed to realize that subprime borrowers are different. For example, they need reminders before they make a payment.[42] Simplification also occurred in 2008 when CEO Killinger lumped banks into two categories, those that were "irrational mortgage lenders" (banks that do nothing but make mortgages) and those that weren't "irrational." Even though WaMu was a perfect example of the "irrational" category because of its escalating exposure to bad mortgage loans, Killinger believed that because WaMu was also in the retail banking business (albeit to a slight degree), it was not an irrational lender.[43]

WaMu's claim that subprime lending was a key business line led it to lump together both qualified and less qualified borrowers. This simplification raised the probability that the bank would become a "predatory lender."[44] Managers would now have more incentives to shift qualified buyers from a regular mortgage to a more profitable subprime loan. Whenever Killinger presented cautionary warnings to the board, he never used the word *bubble* to describe the housing market.[45] This is in contrast with chief risk officer Jim Vanasek, who wrote a memo to his underwriting and appraisal staff in 2004 that urged them to be much more conservative given the continuing rise in housing prices to unsustainable levels: "There have been so many warnings of a Housing Bubble that we all tend now to ignore them because thus far it has not happened."[46]

WaMu also tended to lump together all of its subprime borrowers. This simplification concealed a dangerous set of details. Kevin Jenne, a market research manager, videotaped 80 hours of interviews with high-risk borrowers (e.g., people not paying back their loans).[47] What he saw over and over was that borrowers were confused and had no idea of how their option adjustable-rate mortgages (ARMs) worked (e.g., "Well, this small monthly payment, that's how much we pay, right?").[48] In fact, those loans were negatively amortizing loans. If a borrower chose to make the lowest payment, option 4 ("minimum payment"), that amount would cover only part of the interest and none of the principal, and the remaining amount of unpaid interest would be added to the principal.[49] Risk managers viewed these loans as a liability, but accountants treated them as an asset.[50] Payments on an option ARM could jump from $800 per month to $3,000 per month.[51]

Sensitivity to Operations   The big picture in HROs is just as operational as it is strategic. Anomalies are noticed while they are still tractable and can still be isolated and dealt with. Sensitivity to operations is about the work itself, about seeing what we are actually doing regardless of intentions, designs, and plans. Differences in sensitivity are evident, for example, in interpretations of close calls. Reliable performance tends to increase when close calls are interpreted as danger in the guise of safety and to decrease when close calls are deemed as safety in the guise of danger. Both interpretations are sensitive to what is currently happening but differ greatly in their grasp of operational risk and context. Operations are in jeopardy when their soundness is overestimated. When people see a near miss as success, this reinforces their beliefs that current operations are sufficient to forestall unintended consequences.

Top management's eagerness to acquire firms affected operations at WaMu. The CEO wanted WaMu to be "a category killer" (e.g., the Walmart of banking).[52] This might have been a plausible strategy except that WaMu neglected the firms that it acquired.[53] The highest priority was to make more loans, not to integrate systems. For example, files were erased to make room for new files, and the files themselves were not centralized in one place.[54] Mortgage payments were stored in boxes, unrecorded, and people who paid regularly were treated as if they had defaulted on their loans.[55] Those who paid on time were charged an additional penalty. Hundreds of people complained that the bank not only lost their payments but also charged penalties for its mistakes. Bank personnel tended to minimize the errors, explaining that they reflected "nothing more than mistakes that will, from time to time, occur in the ordinary course of any enterprise."[56]

Management was slow to merge the underwriting operations and the payment servicing systems of the acquired firms.[57] A closer look at the underwriting process showed numerous instances of reliance on stated income, incorrect signatures, documents with sections obscured by correction fluid, and loans for the full amount of the purchase price, all of which were made worse by inexperienced personnel and a relentless push for a greater volume of sales. In the final report of the Senate committee investigating the financial crisis, there is this summary statement: "The records reviewed by the subcommittee showed that from 2004 until its shuttering in 2008, WaMu constantly struggled with information technology issues that limited its ability to monitor loan errors, exception rates, and indicators of loan fraud."[58]

Operations also suffered because of high turnover of bank personnel. This was especially true of employees whose job was to monitor risk or comply with federal regulations.[59] WaMu went through five credit officers in two years.[60] "In March 2007, an OTS[61] examiner noted that WaMu had just hired its 'ninth compliance leader since 2000,' and that its 'compliance management program has suffered a lack of steady, consistent leadership.'"[62] This turnover is not surprising because each risk officer had two bosses, the chief risk officer and the head of the business unit to which he or she was assigned (the policy of double reporting).[63] Given the high priority on sales and growth in each division, the person who oversees risk is in a less powerful position than is the person who oversees the business unit.[64]

Commitment to Resilience   No system is perfect. HROs know this as well as anyone. This is why they complement their anticipatory activities of learning from failure, complicating their perceptions, and remaining sensitive to operations with a commitment to resilience. "The essence of resilience is therefore the intrinsic ability of an organization (system) to maintain or regain a dynamically stable state, which allows it to continue operations after a major mishap and/or in the presence of a continuous stress."[65] HROs develop capabilities to detect, contain, and bounce back from those inevitable errors that are part of an indeterminate world. The hallmark of an HRO is not that it is error-free but that errors don't disable it.

Again, part of the problem at WaMu involved personnel. As new people entered a newer culture devoted to sales and driven by the values of *dynamic* and *driven*, older personnel who were committed to different older values were dismissed as "legacy losers" and "Pepper's misfits."[66] This weakened a commitment to resilience because it reduced the variety of resources available to the firm. Old-timers have different experiences and competencies that are not so much out-of-date as they are diverse resources that may be able to cope with unexpected events.

A subtle trap in WaMu's high-risk strategy can blind people to the ongoing need to develop resilience resources. That trap involves time lags. If subprime borrowers default on their loans, the default won't occur right away, especially if low initial teaser rates attracted them. If borrowers presume erroneously that those rates will continue for the life of the loan, they aren't prepared for a raise in those rates. Initially the strategy will look like it's working. The bank will make money, especially if housing prices continue to rise. But if those trends reverse direction, then a low capability for resilience undermines reliable performance.

Resilience also decreases when loans are issued with multiple layers of risk (risk layering). For example, a loan might be issued to a borrower whose income information was not verified *and* whose loan had a high loan-to-value ratio (often greater than 90 percent, sometimes with the remaining 10 percent loaned by means of a second lien) *and* a low initial interest rate to qualify the borrower in the first place.

Potential resilience, however, did exist. WaMu could originate fewer subprime loans, sell servicing rights, or use other means to off-load risk. Funds were set aside as loss reserves so that the bank could bounce back from unexpected events. But, these reserves were quickly exhausted when loans started to go bad and investors demanded that WaMu repurchase the loans that had defaulted (the securities usually contained a repurchase clause that continued for the life of the loan).[67] WaMu also could have cut the dividend, but with more cash on hand, it would have become a more attractive takeover target.

One of the durable findings in research on HROs is that they distinguish among three modes of operating: normal, up-tempo, and crisis. Resilient actions vary as a function of which operating mode is in effect, but there is seldom any question regarding which mode is currently active. One of the problems at WaMu was considerable variation among units in the urgency of their modes of operating. At higher organizational levels, the prevailing mode of operation was normal (e.g., despite the worsening signs in the subprime market, Killinger wanted to buy another subprime lender, Ameriquest, which would have loaded WaMu up with even more subprime loans).[68] In Killinger's words, "This, frankly, may be one of the best times to take on new loans in our portfolio."[69] Top management treated the situation as normal, but those lower in the hierarchy were far less certain that conditions were normal: "Why isn't he [Killinger] launching us into crisis mode?"[70] If middle management is dealing with a crisis but senior management doesn't recognize this, then people in the middle are using up resilience resources to convert a crisis into something that appears normal. And they are doing so without support or recognition from their superiors. The application of Band-Aids is not a resilient process.

Deference to Expertise   The final distinctive feature of HROs is their deference to expertise. HROs cultivate diversity, not just because it helps them notice more in complex environments, but also because it helps them adapt to the complexities they do spot. Rigid hierarchies have their own unique vulnerability to errors. Errors at higher levels tend to pick up and combine with errors at lower levels, thereby making the resulting problem bigger, harder to comprehend, and more prone to escalation. To prevent this deadly scenario, HROs push decision making down and around.[71] Decisions are made on the front line, and authority migrates to the people with the most expertise, regardless of their rank.

The increasing marginalization of risk officers at WaMu was an indication of reduced deference to expertise. WaMu had a risk mitigation team, but no one in senior management listened to them. In spring 2005, as WaMu moved deeper into a strategy of higher-risk residential loans, the chief risk officer, James Vanasek, sent a note to the executive committee that said in part, "My credit team and I fear that we are considering expanding our risk appetite at exactly the wrong point and potentially walking straight into a regulatory challenge and criticism from both the Street and the Board."[72] The warning went unheeded and not long after, having grown weary of battling the growth of high-risk loans, Vanasek resigned.[73] After he left, "many of his risk management policies were ignored or discarded. For example, by the end of 2007, stated income loans represented 73 percent of

WaMu's Option ARMS, 50 percent of its subprime loans, and 90 percent of its home equity loans."[74] In late 2006, Vanasek's successor, Ron Cathcart, elevated the risk of "residential real estate and mortgage market exposure" to the second-highest risk level at WaMu.[75] Again, the impact of this salient shift in priorities was modest. Warnings had become "noisy" signals because the culture was moving toward the concept that "we are all in sales."[76] If everybody is in sales, then they all interpret weak signals of failure in the context of sales issues. And selling a high-risk loan is a sales win. Furthermore, if your marching orders are "go out and sell," the admonition to "go out and spot risk" makes no sense.

From late 2007 until the bank was seized, the chief enterprise risk manager, Ron Cathcart, was "excluded from Board meetings and calls with investment bankers because he was forthright about WaMu's mortgage loss rates."[77] Recall our earlier mention that, when Cathcart told Killinger that the bank's rating was about to be downgraded, Killinger walked out on him. Also recall our earlier mention that there was high turnover among employees who were experts in monitoring risk, compliance with Federal regulations, and risk mitigation.

As a final example of expertise and WaMu, consider people who issue mortgage insurance. They are experts on risk and have their own underwriting criteria. When Radian Guaranty Inc., an insurance firm, examined a sample of WaMu loans in 2006, it judged the loans "unacceptable" and ineligible for insurance.[78]

What Do We Learn from the WaMu Case?

Our discussion of the demise of WaMu may strike the reader as basically an effortless analysis with a guaranteed moral. Or as it is more commonly described, the analysis is a little like shooting fish in a barrel. We select obvious shortcomings and argue, "You can do better than this."

Actually, we see this differently. We're not trying to *shoot* fish in a barrel; we're trying to *create* fish in a barrel. You won't find fish swimming in distinct barrels in most organizations. And WaMu didn't either. Instead, you'll find fluid situations that stream past you, unlabeled.[79] Typically, one person's fish in a barrel is another person's confusion. Our point is that if you act more like HROs, then you will focus on a set of capabilities that will make surprises more salient, earlier. These capabilities, in the form of five guidelines, form a barrel that puts boundaries around potential threatening events that now become easier to handle. HROs know what to look for, but more crucially they know how to look.

WaMu teaches us that surprises can take several forms. First, surprise can take the form of what Brian Kylen calls "a bolt from the blue."[80] Something appears for which you had no expectation, no prior model of the event, and no hint that it was coming. In the case of WaMu, the hiring of a new CEO 18 days before the bank was closed occurred out of the blue. A second form of surprise occurs when an issue is recognized, but the direction of the expectation is wrong. WaMu expected housing prices to continue their upward trend, but those prices suddenly trended downward. A third form of surprise occurs when you know what will happen, when it will happen, and in what order, but you discover that your timing is off. WaMu salespeople knew that subprime loans were risky and that in some cases they might have to foreclose on the property, but they did not expect that several borrowers would default on their very first payment. A fourth form of surprise occurs when the expected duration of an event proves wrong. When housing prices unexpectedly went down, this was viewed as a temporary correction and not as a bubble that would continue to collapse. A fifth form of surprise occurs when a problem is expected but its amplitude is not. WaMu knew that when it moved more fully into subprime lending, higher gains came with greater risks. But it did not realize that its escalating commitment to this type of loan would produce losses that would bring down the bank.

In each of these five cases of surprise at WaMu, the surprise starts with an expectation. People start with expectations that senior management will not be shuffled in desperation, housing prices will stabilize, defaults will be gradual, corrections will be limited in scale, and strategies will be well thought out. Presumably, if you hold these expectations, you look for evidence that confirms them rather than evidence that disconfirms them. If you find confirming evidence, this "proves" that your hunches about the world are accurate, that you are in control, that you know what's up, and that you are safe. The continuing search for confirming evidence postpones your realization that something unexpected is developing. If you are slow to realize that things are not the way you expected them to be, the problem worsens, becomes harder to solve, and gets entangled with other problems. When it finally becomes clear that your expectation is wrong, there may be few options left to resolve the problem. In the meantime, efficiency and effectiveness have declined, the system is now vulnerable to further collapse, and safety, reputations, and production are on the line.

Just what constitutes a reliability issue in all of this? In this book we treat reliability as a dynamic nonevent. This is shorthand for the idea that ongoing adaptability and a premium on cultivating resilience sustain continuity when performance is threatened by breakdowns. Adaptability and resilience in the face of surprise depend on how units manage weak signals of failure, temptations to simplify, the fine grain of operations, and their usage of expertise. In the case of WaMu, dynamic adapting to environmental changes steadily broke down. The linkages between loan origination and profit were becoming looser, more variable, and less predictable. Management reasoned, if we increase our share of the subprime market, then we'll make more money. But, the bank was not adapting reliably to the worsening of the real estate market, which meant that surprises in the form of increased defaults, delinquencies, and signs of fraud began to increase. The hallmark of reliable performance, dynamic nonevents, was being replaced at WaMu by the more ominous activity of delayed, reactive treatment of unforeseen threats. From the standpoint of reliability, the issue at WaMu is not that more surprises were occurring. Instead, the reliability issue is that resilient action in the face of these mounting surprises decreased.

What does it mean, then, to manage an unexpected event well? Good management of the unexpected is mindful management. By this we mean that people organize themselves in such a way that they are better able to notice the unexpected in the making and halt its development. If they have difficulty halting the development of the unexpected, they focus on containing it. And if the unexpected breaks through the containment, they focus on resilience and swift restoration of system functioning.

By *mindful*, we also mean that systems strive to maintain an underlying style of mental functioning that formulates increasingly plausible interpretations of the context, the problems that define it, and the remedies it contains. The difference between HROs and other organizations is often most evident in the early stages, when the unexpected gives off only weak signals of trouble. The overwhelming tendency is to respond to weak signals with a weak response. Mindfulness preserves the capability to see the significance of weak signals and to respond vigorously.

Conclusion

Organizing is about coordination. And the ways in which coordination is accomplished have a dramatic effect on managing the unexpected. Barry Turner points to the vulnerability inherent in coordinating: "As a caricature, it could be said that organizations achieve a minimal level of co-ordination by persuading their decision-makers to agree that they will all *neglect* the same kinds of consideration when they make decisions."[81] The problem is not with neglect per se. That's unavoidable. The problem instead lies with the innocent-sounding words "persuading," "agree," and "same kinds of consideration." These words all refer to activities that attempt to convert differing concepts and perceptions into ones that are more similar. As this conversion proceeds, neglected differences can become potential sources of disruptive surprise. Mitigation of those surprises depends on variety in sensing and reacting. Intense neglect can undermine that variety. The variety that was available at WaMu to comprehend a changing financial environment steadily decreased as warning signs were dismissed, a singular mission was imposed, personnel were selected for their similarity, divergent voices were silenced, rationales were simplified, and metrics failed to register outliers. None of this shrinkage was mandated. Things could have been otherwise. WaMu is not that different from the organizations in which you participate. All organizations, HROs and non-HROs alike, develop culturally accepted beliefs about the world and its hazards. All organizations develop precautions against these hazards that are set out in norms, regulations, procedures, rules, guidelines, job descriptions, and training materials. And all organizations accumulate unnoticed events that are at odds with accepted beliefs about hazards. These very similarities encourage transfer of the lessons of HROs to other organizations where possible hazards take the form of threats to assets, careers, reputations, legitimacy, credibility, support, trust, or goodwill.

What is striking to us about HROs is that they develop beliefs about the world and its hazards with fewer simplifications, less finality, and more revision than we see in many organizations. The definition of what is hazardous is continually refreshed. And like all organizations, HROs accumulate unnoticed events that are at odds with what they expected, but they tend to notice these accumulated events sooner, when they are smaller. They also concentrate more fully on the anomaly, its meaning, and a recovery that will restore reliable performance. Each of these elaborations of the basics by HROs suggests directions in which other organizations can make their own elaborations in the interest of heightened mindfulness.

Overview of Subsequent Chapters

The remaining chapters cover the following topics. In Chapter 2 we describe the infrastructure of mindful organizing as a combination of expectations, sensemaking, organizing, and managing. These four are explored in the context of efforts by the staff of the Baltimore & Ohio Railroad Museum to manage the collapse of a snow-laden roof onto the artifacts of its world-famous collection. In Chapters 3 through 7 we take a closer look at failure, simplification, operations, resilience, and expertise, one principle at a time. In each of these five chapters, we examine nuances that are implicit in the principle, describe ways to observe its operation, and suggest implications of those observations for practice. Chapter 8, built on successes and failures in the reliability culture at Toyota, spells out how organizational cultures can be produced, lost, recovered, and maintained by mindful organizing. In Chapter 9 we summarize recurring ideas in the book.

2

The Infrastructure of Mindful Organizing

"Organizing tries to ensure that different things are where we expect them to be."[1]

—Yiannis Gabriel

Often, things are not where we expect them to be. When that happens we strive for "a minimum of jolt, a maximum of continuity."[2] That takes a lot more than failure, simplification, operations, resilience, and expertise (FSORE). It takes an infrastructure that supports sensemaking, continuous organizing, and adaptive managing. We lump these three together under the more general label *mindful organizing*, which, for us, means essentially the same thing as high reliability organizing. In both cases we want to convey the image that reliable organizations are sensitive to and constantly adjust to small cues or mishaps that if left unaddressed, could accumulate and interact with other parts of the system resulting in larger problems.[3] Our intent is to suggest a picture of collective mental functioning that is distinguished by continuous updating and deepening of increasingly plausible interpretations of what the context is, what disruptions define it, and what remedies it contains. All of this occurs while people are acting to better comprehend what they notice.

A crucial linkage with other relevant work on reliability is created by the word *comprehend*. Charles Perrow anticipated our focus on mindful organizing[4] when he argued that interactive complexity and tight coupling in systems made it hard to comprehend what was happening when unexpected problems began to enlarge. We reasoned that if some organizational forms could impede comprehension, other forms could facilitate it. Observations of organizations that operate under trying conditions with few accidents suggested that complexity became more comprehensible and manageable when people focused at least as much on processes that sustained performance as on those that increased efficiency. This shift, dubbed high reliability organizing,[5] helped people catch problems earlier, when it took fewer resources to fix them. Furthermore, since the problems were smaller when they were detected, people had a better chance of fixing them completely.

The infrastructure of managing by mindful organizing is illustrated by a set of disruptive events at the Baltimore & Ohio (B&O) Railroad Museum in Baltimore, Maryland.[6] During a severe snowstorm in February 2003,[7] much of the roof of the roundhouse housing the museum's priceless collection of railroad equipment collapsed onto the collection. The roof collapse occurred while the museum was in the midst of preparing for a major international exhibition called the Fair of the Iron Horse. This large fund-raising event was planned for July 2003 to commemorate the one hundred seventy-fifth anniversary of the birth of American railroading. But, the record snowfall, the roof collapse, the destruction of artifacts, the cancellation of the impending Fair, and the discovery of additional unexpected damage late in the rebuild all created a managerial nightmare. This nightmare is a true test of an organization's capability to "respond in real time, reorganizing resources and actions to maintain functioning despite peripheral failures."[8] In this example we see an organizational microcosm of disruptive surprises and the ways in which a unit recovers. What we see in this microcosm are activities of sensemaking, organizing, and managing that were under way. What we suggest is that these three constitute a significant context that shapes whether FSORE is sufficient to maintain reliable performance.

Overview of the Collapse and Recovery

The museum was originally part of the B&O Railroad, the first railroad in the United States (established in 1827), and it became an independent, nonprofit, educational institute in 1990. Much of the museum's collection is located in a building called the roundhouse, which was constructed in 1884. The roundhouse is a 22-sided polygon containing 22 engine bays and a turning mechanism in the center of the building that allows a single worker to rotate a 64-ton locomotive 360 degrees and place it in a bay for repair (see Figure 2.1).[9]

Since 1990, the B&O Railroad Museum—like many other museums—had been struggling financially and had been running deficits for several years. The museum's primary visitors were schoolchildren on class trips and railroad buffs. The 120 volunteers (many of whom were retired railroad employees) far outnumbered the 28 full-time staff, and there were few incentives to increase the numbers at the door.

FIGURE 2.1 B&O Railroad Museum Before the Roof Collapse
(Used with permission of the B&O Railroad Museum)

In 2000, the museum's chief curator, Courtney Wilson, was appointed executive director with an explicit mandate to reduce the deficit. To do this, Wilson envisioned a unique event to celebrate the one hundred seventy-fifth anniversary of American railroading, the Fair of the Iron Horse. The original Fair, held in 1927 to commemorate the centennial anniversary of the B&O Railroad, had been the largest gathering of vintage and current railroad cars in the world.[10] Over a period of two weeks, more than 2 million visitors attended the original Fair, viewing famous locomotives and rolling stock from the B&O Railroad's historic collection and from collections around the world.[11] Given the success of the original Fair, Wilson believed a recreation of the Fair would increase the museum's revenue, public exposure, and international recognition.

A year and a half into preparations, Wilson's plan appeared to be working. But then disaster struck. Over the Presidents' Day weekend in February 2003, a record snowstorm dumped more than two feet of snow on the city of Baltimore. At 2:30 AM on Monday morning, February 17, the museum's director of facilities, Steven Johnson, received notification that an alarm was sounding at the roundhouse. Venturing out in the storm, Johnson soon learned that two of the roundhouse's 22 roof sections had collapsed under the weight of the snow. The collapse damaged the gas system and triggered the sprinklers, which poured 6 inches of water on the museum's collection. Although the museum's senior management realized that something had gone wrong, it wasn't until daylight that they could see just how much damage there was. The roof continued to cave in section by section, and by the midmorning on February 17, the spectacular, cathedral-like roundhouse stood with half its circular roof gone and the railroad collection it held damaged by roof debris, snow, and water (see Figures 2.2 and 2.3).

FIGURE 2.2 Devastation (Used with permission of the B&O Railroad Museum)

FIGURE 2.3 Devastation (Used with permission of the B&O
Railroad Museum)

In the days following the roundhouse collapse, senior management and the board of directors discussed whether the
museum would be able to survive the catastrophe. The collapse
of the roundhouse not only meant that the building and artifacts
were damaged but also that the Fair would have to be cancelled,
which would result in a loss of the almost 1 million dollars already
invested in preparations.[12]

The decision to rebuild the roundhouse was made within the
first week at an emergency meeting of the board of directors and
communicated to the public via a press release on February 28.[13]
To manage the rebuilding effort, Wilson hired engineering,
architectural, and contracting firms headed by individuals who
also sat on the museum's board. He also reorganized the staff into
three departments: Administration and Development (which
focused on fund-raising), Facilities and Security (which helped
facilitate the temporary quarters the staff set up), and Operations

(which focused on storing and cataloguing damage to artifacts). The museum's first goal was to stabilize the roundhouse and determine the extent of its damage. One month passed before the building was stable enough to allow nonconstruction personnel to enter safely. At this point, forensic architects determined that the entire lower roof had been damaged by the storm and would need to be replaced.

Furthermore, portions of the roundhouse's brick walls were damaged and required reinforcement until later reconstruction efforts were possible. Once it was safe to enter the building, artifact handlers began to remove collection pieces. Curatorial staff catalogued and stabilized the damaged artifacts. Artifacts that could not be removed because of size were protected by the erection of scaffolding and screening.

While stabilization and recovery efforts proceeded, the rest of the museum staff focused on funding the recovery. A significant source of money for rebuilding would come from the museum's insurance. Wilson turned to fund-raising, soliciting donations from corporations, and city, state, and federal governments, ultimately gathering $6.25 million with another $1.5 million coming from private donors. Six months postcollapse, the museum finally learned the extent of the resources they would have to rebuild. The roundhouse was insured for the total cost of structural damage caused by the roof collapse. But the collection itself was insured for only $5 million, far less than the projected cost of repairs. The museum dealt with this shortfall by using the $5 million to build a state-of-the-art train restoration and repair facility on the museum campus. Such a facility would not only allow engines and cars damaged by the roof collapse to be repaired but also provide a facility that could restore future items for the museum, repair equipment for other museums that routinely outsourced their reconstruction, and be used as a tour attraction.

Months later, with the roof repair almost complete, a new unexpected event occurred. The museum's intact upper clerestory roof and lantern were declared structurally unsound and required replacement. The upper roof was not covered by insurance. Its repair would cost $2 million and add an extra six months onto the construction period, which meant that the business interruption insurance would run out before the project was completed.

The museum also had to determine whether to bring the roundhouse and the rest of the museum's buildings up to code (for example, because of their national landmark status, the museum was not required to comply with the Americans with Disabilities Act during rebuilding). This question, combined with the other challenges, prompted the museum to reconsider basic assumptions underlying the rebuild process. People realized that they could take advantage of the temporary cessation of operations not just to restore what had existed before but also to rethink what would make the museum appeal to a wider public.

The museum that finally reopened on November 13, 2004, was considerably changed from the museum that Wilson had inherited (see Figure 2.4). The museum was now much larger (exhibit space increased by 72,245 square feet), it focused on a wider audience of museumgoers (families as well as railroad buffs), it offered better access (e.g., making the museum wheelchair accessible also improved access for families with children in strollers), and it presented more exhibits and activities (e.g., a living history and demonstration center).[14] Culturally, the organization was no longer as severely siloed. Museum staff described the museum's transformation from an organization where curatorial and administrative staff rarely interacted to an organization where staff communicated freely with one another and where the long-standing tension between the curators and administrators had decreased.

FIGURE 2.4 B&O Railroad Museum Fully Restored (Used with permission of the B&O Railroad Museum)

The Unexpected and the Expected

None of these events was expected. Instead, the B&O Railroad Museum personnel expected that the Fair would open as scheduled, raise money, increase public visibility, broaden international recognition, recruit supporters who were more active, and give the museum a higher profile. But, without warning, the personnel suddenly faced a damaged building, splintered rail cars, no jobs, 30 catered events scheduled, a rail fair scheduled to open in five months for which they had already started selling tickets, a formal kickoff of the Fair scheduled for February 27 (the collapse was February 17), and fair souvenirs that were later sold off at train shows, and as if this weren't enough, the museum's only copies of its disaster plans were in desks buried under the rubble.

Unexpected events occur mostly because we create organizations that construct and enact expected events in the first place.[15] To have an expectation is to envision something, usually for good reasons, that is reasonably certain to come about.[16] To expect something is to be mentally ready for it. Almost every deliberate action you take is based on assumptions about how the world will react to what you do. "Expectancies form the basis for virtually all deliberate actions because expectancies about how the world operates serve as implicit assumptions that guide behavioral choices."[17] Expectations direct your attention to certain features of events, which means that they affect what you notice, mull over, and remember.

John Dewey summarized this sequence when he said, "In every waking moment, the complete balance of the organism and its environment is constantly interfered with and as constantly restored . . . Life is interruptions and recoveries . . . At these moments of a shifting of activity, conscious feeling and thought arise and are accentuated."[18]

That "accentuation" of thought and feeling when interruptions occur is apparent in Courtney Wilson's reflections: "I've had an experience that forced me to look at the core values of the institution. Why were we created? What is our mission? Do we have the capability to survive this disaster? And is the mission and the money it's going to take to do it worth it? . . . We lose the roundhouse. I still have four other historic buildings. I still have the body of a pretty phenomenal collection. What do I do? Do I tear the roundhouse down completely or do I put up a modern building? What difference would that make in the future of the museum?"[19] What Wilson describes is an instance where limited conceptions clash with unlimited interdependencies.

Recall the epigraph at the beginning of this chapter: Organizing *ensures* that different things are where we *expect* them to be. If expectations are that central, then managing amid those expectations has its own logic. As organizational scholar Barbara Czarniawska explains it, "Management is mindful when it is aware of its own expectations, the limited horizon of these expectations, and the need for ongoing corrections."[20] If, however, expectations are unnoticed, unconstrained, and untouchable, then systems become more vulnerable. To clarify, bound, and update expectations is to reduce the disruption that unexpected events produce.

Sensemaking

The ongoing disruptions of museum events are partly a story of flux and hunches. Flux involves continuing change, fluctuation, and flow. However, the experience of flux is usually short-lived because it gets converted into hunches. Once hunches are imposed, flux "flows as if shot through with adjectives and nouns and prepositions and conjunctions."[21] These substitutions of words for flux are necessary to get things done. And these substitutions are inevitable. *"The intellectual life of man consists in his substitution of a conceptual order for the perceptual order in which his experience originally comes."*[22] These substitutions are prominent in sensemaking.

The act of substituting discontinuous concepts for continuous perceptions is mutually reinforcing. Concepts give meaning to perceptions and perceptions give substance to concepts. That exchange is basic to managing the unexpected since a breakdown in either connection can produce disabling surprises. If perception occurs without some kind of connection to concepts, then the perception is blind (e.g., "What's going on here, and where is here?"). Something is flowing past us, but we have no way to bracket it, assign it to a type, or know how to deal with it. But it is also the case that concepts that are not connected to perceptions are empty (e.g., "Are we a railroad archive if we have nothing to archive?"). Empty concepts occur when we have a headful of types, labels, and abstractions but no specifics that fit them.[23] Basic to any attempt at managing the unexpected are changes that either make empty concepts fuller by anchoring them in perceptions or make blind perceptions more meaningful by linking them with plausible, differentiated concepts. When concepts and perceptions coevolve, fuller concepts produce more meaningful perceptions, which in turn fill out and fine-tune concepts, which further improves perception, noticing, and attunement to flux and incipient surprises. Whether such coevolution occurs and is maintained depends on how people make sense, organize, and manage.

When people are thrown into moments of nonobviousness, their questions are "What's the story here" and "Now what?" They usually ask these questions while they keep acting. This is what we mean by sense*making*. Sensemaking is about sizing up a situation while you simultaneously act and partially determine the nature of what you discover. Sensemaking, in other words, is seldom an occasion for passive diagnosis. Instead, it is usually an attempt to grasp a developing situation in which the observer affects the trajectory of that development.

We see all of this vividly in a crucial board meeting at the museum that was held shortly after the roof collapse. As the meeting convened, portions of the roof were still collapsing, the structure was becoming more unstable, and much of the collection was becoming more and more waterlogged. The collapse itself still had no meaning and made no sense. But, the board changed that when it decided, "We're going to reopen! We're going to put everything back together." *Better than ever* was its new strategy. The museum website was retitled "Restoration Reports." And the future museum was now called an "attraction" to underscore how the new experience would be more family friendly.

At this board meeting, management turned circumstances into a situation that was comprehended explicitly in words that served as a springboard for action.[24] The word *circumstances* is just another name for flux. And when you comprehend flux and turn it into a situation, you rely on words, categories, and descriptions that serve as a springboard to action (e.g., "We're going to reopen"). When we make sense, we turn continuous perceptions into discontinuous concepts, a finite number of types, and descriptions that we can meaningfully share. Sensemaking is a social process that edits, abridges, simplifies, and brackets our firsthand experience with flux. And the social character of sensemaking determines how well the unexpected can be managed.

A crucial dynamic in social sensemaking is what social psychologists Reuben Baron and Stephen Misovich have labeled the "shareability constraint."[25] They argue that sensemaking develops from knowledge by acquaintance that comes from active exploration. Active exploration involves perceptually based, hands-on, and detail-driven cognitive processing to take action. But, if people want to share their knowledge by acquaintance with others, then that knowledge has to take on a different form.[26] When people share their knowledge they shift from perceptually based knowing to categorically based knowing in order to coordinate their actions. Now they develop knowledge by description rather than knowledge by acquaintance, their cognitive processing becomes concept-driven rather than perception-driven, and they go beyond the information given and convert their direct perceptions into types, categories, routines, and roles. Remember, concept-driven processing runs the risk of being empty, ungrounded, and too general to single out the specifics of an unexpected event. And perception-driven processing runs the risk of being blind, undifferentiated, and too singular to suggest a pattern. Either way, people know less and less. The goal in managing the unexpected is to facilitate conversations of acquaintance rather than conversations edited solely by description.

There are ways to work within the shareability constraint as will become clearer when we discuss mindful organizing. By way of preview, we can combine acquaintance and description if collectively people (1) actively differentiate and refine their existing descriptions; (2) create new, distinct categories and descriptions out of the continuous streams of events that flow through their activities; and (3) develop a more nuanced appreciation of the context of events and of alternative ways to preserve that context in their interpretations.[27] This combination of differentiation, creation, and appreciation captures more details, evokes a wider variety of roles, and synthesizes those details and rules into richer shared conjectures.

Throughout this book we mention sensemaking more often than we mention decision making. Sensemaking constructs the circumstances that then may seem to require a decision. But the decision is incidental since the meaning of the situation has already been sufficiently fixed so that it affords a next step. Decision making consists mainly of the ratification of a sense of the situation that has already been defined, constrained, and framed interactively. Thus, when people talk about good decision making and how to make better decisions, they are really talking about occasions when people interact to identify and validate mutually compatible versions of what the story is and what to do next.

A durable way of depicting organizations that blends decision making and sensemaking is the following:

An alternative perspective [to that of the rational organization] on organizations holds that *information* is limited and serves largely to *justify decisions* or *positions* already taken; *goals*, *preferences* and effectiveness *criteria* are *problematic* and conflicting; organizations are loosely linked to their social environments; the *rationality* of various *designs* and *decisions* is *inferred* after the fact to *make sense* out of things that have already happened; organizations are coalitions of various *interests*; organization designs are frequently *unplanned* and are basically responses to contests among interests for control over the organization; and organization designs are in part *ceremonial*. This alternative perspective attempts explicitly to recognize the social nature of organizations.[28]

The italicized words highlight ways in which decision making is dependent on and constrained by sensemaking.

Organizing and Collective Sensemaking

As we just saw, sensemaking and organizing are interrelated. Yiannis Gabriel describes that relationship this way: "Organizing is a constant sensemaking process, a constant effort to impose order on our perceptions, experiences, and expectations."[29]

Organizing creates patterns and order in flux. The phrase *high reliability organization* can be misleading because it suggests a static container rather than a dynamic activity. That's why we use the phrase *high reliability organizing* to describe ongoing, collective efforts to improve and maintain reliability. When we say that an activity is organized, we mean the same thing that organizational scholar Hari Tsoukas means by the word *organized*: To call an activity organized "implies that *types* of behaviour in *types* of situations are connected to *types* of actors . . . An organized activity provides actors with a given set of *cognitive categories* and a *typology* of action options . . . On this view, therefore, organizing implies *generalizing*; the *subsumption of heterogeneous particulars under generic categories*. In that sense, formal organization necessarily involves *abstraction*."[30]

Tsoukas captures several nuances of the words *organization* and *organizing*. The italicized words illustrate how cognitively demanding organizing can be. This suggests that depicting situations in explicit words is a crucial tool in managing the unexpected.

Inputs that do not fit into types tend to be treated as insignificant. Tsoukas also is clear that it is activities, not structures, that are organized. Any organization's dominant categories affect the action options that people consider. And the glue, so to speak, that holds organizations and environments together consists largely of concepts, categories, and generalizations.

Given the dynamic quality of organizing, it is tough to locate just what "*the* organization" consists of. To make it easier, think about organizational communication and the conversations that embody much of it. Think of those distributed conversations as the *site* where organization emerges. And think of the things that people talk about at those sites as the textual *surfaces* from which the organization's substance is read. If we set up organizing this way, then organizations are talked into existence (sites), they gain their substance from the content of the discussions that are produced there (surfaces), and they "become" the organization when macro actors summarize and speak on behalf of a sample of these conversations (e.g., "The WaMu way is to be driven!"). These conversations create organizational reality; they don't just represent an entity that is already there.

For an organization to act, its knowledge must undergo two transformations: (1) That knowledge has to be preserved in texts that retain distributed understandings; (2) that knowledge has to be voiced by someone who speaks on behalf of the network and its knowledge.[31] We describe organizing this way to animate early examples of HROs (e.g., aircraft carriers) that seemed to be basically well-structured bureaucracies. In those bureaucracies reliable performance was often attributed to structures formed by rules, formal procedures, hierarchical positions, regulations, and fixed plans as well as self-organizing networks of expertise.

These bureaucratic forms remain important these days, but our intent is to summarize principles that are less tied to such forms. Organizations in recent decades retain many vestiges of bureaucracy, but they also tend to be "smaller (as far as number of employees go), flatter, looser, more international, more flexible, less centralized, more likely to be in partnerships with other organizations, less pyramid-like, and more network-like."[32] To describe managing the unexpected under these less permanent conditions is to rely more heavily on ways in which people are guided by cognitive categories and typologies, by loosely connected conversations and texts, by intermittent collective summaries voiced by spokespeople, and by a heavier reliance on trust.

Given these looser configurations, there is no question that trust is crucial for organizing.[33] But trust itself tends to be oversimplified. The concepts of trust and dynamic organizing become more relevant to practice if we adopt a set of conventions social scientist Donald Campbell first discussed.[34] In everyday life we all use our own experience to get a better idea of what is going on, and we also rely on the experience of others. This is all well and good *until* those shared experiences seem to conflict. Then we have the problem of what weights to put on our own viewpoint and what weights to put on others' viewpoints. Since our viewpoints have their limits, we can't afford to ignore completely what others think is happening. But the other people can't afford to ignore us either. Therefore, if we want to combine our observations with those of other people, and maintain our ability to adapt to change, we have to do three things:

1. We have to *trust* the reports of others and be willing to base our beliefs and actions on them;

2. We have to report *honestly* so that others can use our observations to help them come to valid beliefs; and

3. We have to maintain *self-respect*, which means we have to respect our own perceptions and beliefs and seek to integrate them with the reports of others without belittling either them or ourselves.

Reporting honestly turns out to be much tougher in hierarchical organizations than people admit.[35] Problems with trustworthiness and honest reporting will show up repeatedly throughout this book.

In the recovery of the B&O Railroad Museum, conversations, new categories, adapting, and trust were abundant. For example, there were daily calls from insurers and from public insurance adjustment companies who wanted to handle the museum's claims. Hiring a public adjustment firm for such a large claim would have been the conventional approach to such a situation. But, the director of development and sponsorship programs (who later became the chief operating officer), had worked in her father's certified public accountant office while she was growing up. Based on this and her previous experience negotiating with vendors and sponsors in preparing for the Fair, she felt she could handle the claims. Wilson agreed with her assessment and gave her the job. The adjusting activity was sustained reliably, and the outcomes contributed to a stronger museum when it reopened.

The important point in these otherwise commonplace changes is that organizing keeps being reaccomplished. The organization keeps drifting toward disorganization and organizing keeps rebuilding it. The recovering museum never was a stable entity. Instead, ongoing processes of stabilizing, reorganizing, reimagining, and routinizing reconstituted it. *The* museum was the fiction, not the processes that propped up the fiction.

Adaptive Managing

Sensemaking and organizing are human activities that are jointly managed in the interest of sustained reliable performance. When we use the word *managing*, we mean, "Managing is firstly and fundamentally the task of attending to, sorting out, and prioritizing an inherently messy world of competing demands that are placed on a manager's attention . . . Active perceptual organization and the astute allocation of attention is a central feature of the managerial task."[36] The reason this description anchors our analysis is because it highlights the confrontation with a messy world (flux), the recurrence of competing demands (expectations), perceptual organization through sorting out demands and prioritizing them (sensemaking), and the centrality of attention as a design principle in collective action (organizing).

Because of its relevance to sensemaking, managing the unexpected is often facilitated when managers provide their own view of the current situation, the task, their own intentions, cues that could signal a situational change, and a request for added input. The acronym for this protocol, summarized by psychologist Gary Klein,[37] is STICC: situation, task, intent, concerns, and calibrate. Converted into words, the protocol would sound like this:

1. The Situation = Here's what I think we face.
2. The Task = Here's what I think we should do.
3. The Intent = Here's why I think that is what we should do.
4. The Concerns = Here's what we should keep our eye on because if that changes, we're in a whole new ball game.
5. Calibrate = Now talk to me. (Some groups elaborate this fifth step into three specific requests: Tell me if you (a) don't understand, (b) can't do it, or (c) see something I don't.)

Once you pose a forthcoming situation in these terms, it becomes more meaningful. Equally important, it is now easier for people to spot the unexpected because they have a clearer idea of what to expect. In step 4, you say essentially, "Look, the situation may change, expectations may not be fulfilled, the unexpected could happen, and we may need to update our expectations, so watch out for that possibility."

Think back to the situation that Wilson had to manage at the museum after the roof collapse. Top management had to manage the passions of the board looking for explanations, the curators looking for objects, the staff looking for work, the dedicated volunteers looking for rubble to shovel, and the press looking for screwups. In Wilson's view it was crucial that above all else he remain "a nonanxious presence" and prioritize unprioritized input. As Wilson put it, "The worst part of it was watching the pain—not showing my pain—but watching the pain of my curators' faces day after day, seeing an African American porter's uniform from 1899 sitting on a twisted mannequin and getting rained and snowed on and they knew it was one of only two that existed from that period in America and standing outside and looking in and wanting so badly to run in and having me grab them by the collar and say, 'No, you don't.'"[38]

Despite all of these competing demands, the museum kept functioning. And it did so through a combination of sensemaking, organizing, and managing. The staff maintained the curating function of preserving artifacts, but the curating was done by iron workers. The staff also maintained the preservation function because they kept acting as people to whom valuable artifacts had been entrusted. They exhibited unexpected ingenuity in improvising ways to continue curating and preserving the artifacts. For example, in the first month after the collapse, when only steel workers were allowed to enter the unstable space, the staff had to decide which pieces of rubble could be thrown away and which needed to be saved. The curators trained the steel workers in the basics of curating. Wilson described the restructuring this way:

Ultimately the steel workers that were in the building—we got the curators outside with binoculars and walkie-talkies and they said, "Okay. Get a pair of gloves. That's an artifact. Now take it careful," and they were coaching them. And the steel workers were bringing the artifacts out. And it was funny. When they were cleaning the rubble out, the slate and the iron and the snow, they were in there and they would find something that didn't look like a piece of slate. And they'd go, "Hey!" And they'd hold it up in the air and the curator would be outside, a hard hat on and freezing to death and go, "That's crap! Throw it away." Or, "No! That's good! Bring it to me."[39]

Museum staff were able to get a grip soon after the collapse because that's what they had been doing all along. We sometimes refer to these daily activities as *putting out fires*. And when we do so, we sometimes see this as a sign of poor managing. However, firefighting may strengthen rather than weaken resilience because it gives people multiple experiences with coping and closure. Another way to describe repeated experiences of coping and closure is to describe them as strengthening, the capability not to be overwhelmed. That capability may come from learning that experiences of interruption are accompanied by manageable anxiety, finite duration, and acceptable recovery. For example, while preparing for the Fair, staff members learned how to make do with limited resources, recover from small-scale interruptions, restructure their short-term goals, analyze what they had and what they needed, and relate to people who were strangers but controlled key resources. Critical learnings such as these helped the staff handle other novel events. Later, when the roof collapsed, these prior learnings likely made it possible for the system to degrade more gracefully and to recover more effectively. Perhaps the ultimate prioritizing was Wilson's reassurance: "Look, we're just a museum; no one is going to die or go hungry if we close tomorrow."[40]

A Concluding Assessment

Effective managing of the unexpected basically converts the flux of demands, anomalies, and uncertainties into a more orderly set of action-based hunches about failure, simplification, operations, resilience, and expertise. And this conversion is a joint product of sensemaking, organizing, and managing. That description fits the case of the B&O museum, in both the preparation for the Fair and the managing after the roof collapse. In both instances, even though the interpretations neglected a host of details, they still preserved some knowledge by acquaintance.

The B&O museum experienced at least three significant interruptions. First, the daily activities of the museum staff were interrupted by the one-off preparations for the upcoming Fair of the Iron Horse. Second, preparations for the Fair were interrupted when the roof of the roundhouse collapsed and crushed significant artifacts. Third, the scheduled reopening of the museum after the roundhouse reconstruction was interrupted by newly discovered damage to the clerestory upper roof. In each case organizing routines, modified while coping with previous interruptions, helped the staff create order in subsequent events. For example, in coping with each interruption, museum personnel repeatedly built enduring relationships in the face of increasingly varied demands (e.g., media asking questions in search of scandals) that were imposed by more varied constituents (e.g., insurance brokers, legislators, iron workers trained as substitute curators) and with increasingly varied stakes (e.g., Will we continue as an attraction? Will we continue with the showcase roundhouse? Will we continue as an archive?). Although the incitements were increasingly diverse, learning tied those diverse demands to a smaller, recurring set of organizing activities. As a result, disruptions were managed toward greater continuity of effort through learning.[41]

How well does each of the following statements describe your work unit, department, or organization? Enter next to each item below the number that corresponds with your conclusion: 1 = not at all, 2 = to some extent, 3 = a great deal.

1. We have a good "map" of each other's talents and skills.　　　　　　　_____

2. We talk about mistakes and ways to learn from them.　　　　　　　_____

3. We discuss our unique skills with each other so we know who has relevant specialized skills and knowledge.　　　　　　　_____

4. We discuss alternatives as to how to go about our normal work activities.　　　　　　　_____

5. When discussing emerging problems with coworkers, we usually discuss what to look out for.　　　　　　　_____

6. When attempting to resolve a problem, we take advantage of the unique skills of our colleagues.　　　　　　　_____

7. We spend time identifying activities we do not want to go wrong.　　　　　　　_____

8. When errors happen, we discuss how we could have prevented them.　　　　　　　_____

9. When a crisis occurs, we rapidly pool our collective expertise to attempt to resolve it.　　　　　　　_____

Scoring: Add the numbers. If you score higher than 22, your firm's *mindful organizing* practices are strong. If you score between 14 and 21, your firm's mindful organizing practices are moderate. Scores lower than 14 suggest that you should actively be thinking of ways to improve your firm's mindful organizing practices.

FIGURE 2.5 The Mindfulness Organizing Scale

What makes the museum story even more intriguing is that, in the final analysis, the original goals for the Fair were actually achieved. As the museum moved toward reopening, there were more funds, more public exposure, more international recognition, larger crowds, a higher profile, more competent staff, and a larger set of loyal supporters. Staging the Fair of the Iron Horse and managing it as a large event is not all that different from staging a museum recovery and managing as if it were a large event. If you get better at one, you get better at the other.[42]

But where do you stand now? With the examples of WaMu and the B&O Railroad Museum in mind, you might be wondering about your own organization's capabilities to manage surprises and sustain reliable performance. An economical way to obtain an overview of those capabilities is to use an audit created by Vanderbilt management professor Tim Vogus (see Figure 2.5).[43] The basics of FSORE are tapped in the questions in the figure. If you complete this audit and ask others in your organization to do the same, you could get a better sense of the current fit between your efforts and those made by organizations that put a premium on reliability as well as efficiency.

3

Principle 1: Preoccupation with Failure

"As soon as a person begins any action whatsoever, the action starts to escape from his intentions, it enters a sphere of interactions and is finally grasped by the environment in a way that may be contrary to the initial intention."[1]

—Edgar Morin

A s actions begin to escape from intentions, they usually don't do so suddenly. Instead, they generate a series of emerging cues that suggest escaping is under way. And noticing these subtle changes as they unfold is the object of a preoccupation with failure. Preoccupations with failure are evident in this sample of overheard comments focused on reliability:

1. "We haven't made that mistake that way before."
2. "Once you've seen one, you've seen one."
3. "If something dumb, dangerous, or different comes up, interrupt me in the cockpit."
4. "The emergency pressure release worked."
5. "It was a routine refinery fire."

The first three statements reflect an alertness, understanding, and wariness that seems missing from the last two. In the last two cases the incident should not have gotten that far. It did so because defenses were breached, weak signals were ignored, and anomalies were treated as normal.

Preoccupation with failure, the first high reliability organization (HRO) principle, captures the need for continuous attention to anomalies that could be symptoms of larger problems in a system. HROs are preoccupied with failure in three ways. First, they work hard to detect small, emerging failures because these may be a clue to additional failures elsewhere in the system. Second, HROs work hard to anticipate and specify significant mistakes that they don't want to make. Third, HROs know that people's knowledge of the situation, the environment, and their own group is incomplete. When people look for failures, they acknowledge the existence of incomplete knowledge.[2]

Components of Preoccupation with Failure

This first principle is more complicated than it might seem. The complications center on anomalies, cues, normalizing, wariness, and doubt.

Anomaly

Failure presumes a lot of prior knowledge. Otherwise, how would you know whether a change represents failing? The word *anomaly* is important in this context because it refers to a cue that does not fit into a series, something that is a departure from common order, form, or rule.[3] William James suggests that such cues take the form of "contrasts in the quality of the successive segments of the stream of thought."[4] Examples are common. The panel investigating the Columbia shuttle disaster concluded, "NASA's system for tracking anomalies for flight readiness reviews failed."[5] Richard Cook and David Woods found that anesthesia accidents in surgical teams occur when "evidence discrepant from the agent's or team's current assessment is missed or discounted or rationalized as not really being discrepant with the current assessment."[6] What's important about this first principle is that its application magnifies an interruption. It makes the interruption stand out more sharply and for a longer period, both of which make it harder to dismiss or normalize.

Cues of Evolving Failure

Failures evolve, which means that detection involves a judgment that something is fail*ing*. Unfortunately, that may not be apparent until something has already failed. Actions *become* mistaken; their meaning takes time to develop. During this evolving, cues become clues. A cue is something noticed, a sign, whereas a clue is a hunch about what that something means. Both are provisional. Cues, as sociologist Diane Vaughan has argued,[7] tend to be weak, mixed, and routine, which makes them easier to take for granted than to question.

The conversion of a cue into a clue provides emerging evidence that the anomaly is meaningful and potentially significant.

A common moment in conversations about reliability sounds like this: "If I had known back then what I know now, I would have acted differently, but what I see now with the benefit of hindsight was unknown back then." Marianne Paget describes the quality of an emerging mistake: "A mistake follows an act. It identifies the character of an act in its aftermath. It names it. An act, however, is not mistaken; it becomes mistaken. There is a paradox here, for seen from the inside of action that is from the point of view of an actor, an act becomes mistaken only after it has already gone wrong. As it is unfolding, it is not becoming mistaken at all; it is becoming."[8]

"Becoming mistaken" is hard to spot in real time. To be preoccupied with failure is to update deliberately and often. That means you have to remain sensitive to failing, changing, and evolving and to be especially wary of fixation on a singular interpretation.[9] When people are preoccupied with failure, this mitigates fixation. Small anomalies serve as prods to reexamine intentions and expectations. Recall steps 4 and 5 in the situation, task, intent, concerns, and calibrate (STICC) protocol, "concerns" and "calibrate." They incorporate the spirit of HRO principle 1. To express "concern" is to call attention to potential departures from expectation. To "calibrate" is to solicit reports of anomalies that might have been missed.

Normalizing

People live as if their expectations are basically correct and as if little can surprise them. To do otherwise would be to forgo any feeling of control or predictability. That's why managing the unexpected is hard. People in HROs worry a lot about the temptation to treat unexpected events as if they are really no big deal. Vaughan found this tendency to "normalize" the unexpected[10] in her reanalysis of the January 28, 1986, explosion of the Challenger space shuttle. When unexpected burn marks appeared on the O-rings between sections of the booster rockets, engineers kept changing their definition of what was an "acceptable risk." They claimed that it was acceptable for hot gases to leak past the gaskets. What they first treated as an unexpected event they now treated as an expected event. This was not the first such redefinition of acceptable risk. The judgment of what was "normal" went from the judgment that it was normal to have heat on the primary O-ring, to normal to have erosion on the primary O-ring, to normal to have gas blowby, to normal to have blowby reach the secondary O-ring, and finally that it was normal to have erosion on the secondary ring.[11] As the National Aeronautics and Space Administration's (NASA) Larry Wear put it, "Once you've accepted an anomaly or something less than perfect, you know, you've given up your virginity. You can't go back. You're at the point that it's very hard to draw the line. You know, next time they say it's the same problem, it's just eroded five mils more. Once you accepted it, where do you draw the line? Once you've done it, it's very difficult to go back now and get very hard-nosed and say I'm not going to accept that."[12]

Institutionalized Wariness

Failures that include misspecification, misestimating, and misunderstanding[13] have histories that stretch back before their appearance in unexpected events. These histories give off small indications of discrepancies along the way, discrepancies that are easy to spot in hindsight but hard to see at the time. This potential growth of the unexpected leads us to make a different set of assumptions from those associated with the well-known "swiss cheese model" of serious accidents.[14] That model portrays chains of events as holes in separate slices of swiss cheese that line up in such a way that defenses are breached and an accident occurs. Our interest is in the process of lining up over time. Each moment where one hole aligns with another represents a failed expectation. And each failed expectation is also an opportunity to stop the progression.

Worries about failure are functional simply because there are limits to foresight. That is why people in HROs have been described as skeptical, wary, and suspicious of quiet periods. This lingering wariness is especially necessary when people have experienced success. Management professors Bill Starbuck and Frances Milliken spotted several of these liabilities in their analysis of the Challenger disaster: "Success breeds confidence and fantasy. When an organization succeeds, its managers usually attribute success to themselves or at least to their organization, rather than to luck. The organization's members grow more confident of their own abilities, of their manager's skills, and of their organization's existing programs and procedures. They trust the procedures to keep them apprised of developing problems, in the belief that these procedures focus on the most important events and ignore the least significant ones."[15]

Success narrows perceptions, changes attitudes, reinforces a single way of doing things, breeds overconfidence in current practices, and reduces acceptance of opposing points of view. The problem is that if people assume that success demonstrates competence, they are more likely to drift into complacency and inattention. What they don't realize is that complacency also increases the likelihood that unexpected events will go undetected longer and accumulate into bigger problems.

Furthermore, a series of successes without a serious incident may tempt people to change their beliefs about reliability and to move resources elsewhere. "This behavior continues until the agency's estimates of reliability are so high and resources allocated to guarding against failure so low that it is almost inevitable that a failure occurs."[16] The problem here is that reliability hasn't changed. There is no evidence that the probability of failure should be revised downward—and no evidence that the pre-occupation with failure should be relaxed. Instead, a string of successes without failures basically validates the original assessment and defensive routines.[17]

Doubt as a Mind-Set

The word *failing* implies that preoccupation is a dynamic process and that John Dewey's conscious feelings and thoughts that accompany interruptions are dynamic as well.[18] Feelings of doubt are important in managing the unexpected. Here's an example. At the Mary Pang bakery fire in Seattle on January 5, 1995,[19] the incident commander (IC) sent a hose team into the bakery through the front door to keep a presumed external structural fire from entering the building. Because the building was built into a hillside, the IC thought he was sending firefighters in on the bottom floor of a one-story building. In fact, he was sending them in on the second floor of a two-story building. The first floor beneath them was completely involved with fire. The fire burned out supports in a wall that was holding up the second floor, the second floor collapsed, and four firefighters fell into the first floor inferno and lost their lives. One of the more heartbreaking moments of the fire was an incident with a rookie firefighter who was working above the fire on the second floor. The rookie's fire helmet fell off and when he leaned down to pick it up, he felt how hot the concrete floor was. He said to himself, but to no one else, "I have to remember to ask my Captain when we get back to the station, why concrete gets hot. I didn't know that it did." We now know that fire was burning under the crew. In one sense, the rookie knew this. But in another, he didn't know what to make of the strange cue and he didn't ask immediately. As a result, the cue was not recognized as a meaningful clue of danger.

Doubt is crucial in managing the unexpected as Eric-Hans Kramer makes clear in his provocative analysis titled "Organizing Doubt."[20] Kramer probed the often-senseless world of Dutch armed forces assigned to peacekeeping operations in the former Yugoslavia. These units faced the dual problems of not understanding the conflicts well beforehand (no one did) and not knowing what they would encounter on patrols (e.g., shootings, mines, aggressive local population, roadblocks, witnessed atrocities, deplorable living conditions, everyday accidents, and people who did not seem to be in need of help at all). In these crisis operations, units were confronted with unfamiliar tasks, roles, and problems. And their interpretations, of necessity, had to be provisional. Two themes tie together Kramer's analysis. First, "If the environment is dynamically complex it is impossible to know and understand everything in advance, therefore you need to be able to doubt your existing insights."[21] Second, "If the ability to doubt is of crucial importance for organizations dealing with dynamic complexity, organizations need to organize their ability to doubt . . . (A) spirit of contradiction should be organized."[22]

A "spirit of contradiction" is established when people are confronted with different points of view, argumentation and criticism are encouraged, controversy is sought and discussed, and all of this increases the variety that can be mobilized to deal with the unexpected. This contrasts with a "spirit of accord" where sensitive topics are avoided, people use tactics of polite conversation, and "arguers are motivated to present a favorable image of themselves."[23] A current worldview may assist adaptation to the categorized world it envisions, but unless that worldview is both believed and doubted,[24] adaptability to change is lost.

Connotations of Preoccupation with Failure

Some people object to the assertion that one means to manage the unexpected is to be preoccupied with failure. As one operator put it, "If every day we have to assume that we've missed something, then it is a real struggle to think that way." Perhaps it is a struggle, but it's also your job to sustain the flow of reliable work. And part of that job is also to look out for others and not to compound their surprises. For example, managers at NASA avoided this struggle for alertness and contributed to the Columbia shuttle disaster. In the words of the Columbia Accident Investigation Board, "When managers in the Shuttle Program denied the team's request for imagery [of the damaged shuttle], the Debris Assessment Team was put in the untenable position of having to prove that a safety-of-flight issue existed without the very images that would permit such a determination. This is precisely the opposite of how an effective safety culture would act. Organizations that deal with high-risk operations must always have a healthy fear of failure-operations must be proved safe rather than the other way around. NASA inverted the burden of proof."[25]

Systems that seek higher reliability worry chronically that analytic errors are embedded in ongoing activities and that unexpected failure modes and limitations of foresight may amplify those analytic errors. The people who operate and manage HROs "assume that each day will be a bad day and act accordingly. But this is not an easy state to sustain, particularly when the thing about which one is uneasy has either not happened, or has happened a long time ago, and perhaps to another organization."[26] These systems have been characterized as consisting of "collective bonds among suspicious individuals."[27]

A variation of the objection that wariness is a struggle is the objection that managing the unexpected is focused on the negative. As some colleagues have asked, "How does this negative perspective align with the growing attention to positive organizational scholarship (POS)?" The short answer is that managing the unexpected sustains performance so that positive recommendations can then be enacted.

POS, first introduced by our University of Michigan colleagues in 2003,[28] aims to explore especially positive outcomes, processes, and attributes of organizations and their members that contribute to organizational strength and flourishing.

From our perspective, there is nothing especially negative about strengthening the capability to resist threats. Strengthening comes about by organizing in ways to become aware of problems earlier so that they can be remedied before they enlarge and preclude positive dynamics. Breakdowns are inevitable. That's the human condition, it's not just a view through dark-colored glasses. "Human fallibility is like gravity, weather, and terrain—just another foreseeable hazard."[29] As we mentioned earlier, what is striking about the activity of organizing is that our actions usually don't start out mistaken, they become mistaken. And it is that *becoming* that is the focus of this book. An action that is *becoming* mistaken is ambiguous during much of its development. That's why it takes something as strong as a *preoccupation* to spot emerging mistakes when recovery is still possible.

What we want to understand is how units go through a day filled with a million accidents waiting to happen, and at the end of the day, those accidents have not happened. To us, that is an amazing act of positive organizing. What is striking about this outcome is that it occurs in the face of a pervasive tendency toward what sociologist Karen Cerulo calls "positive asymmetry."[30] Positive asymmetry is the cultural tendency of people to focus on and exaggerate the best-case characteristics and the most optimistic outlook or outcomes. This tendency "to see only the best characteristics and potential of people, places, objects, and events" until it is too late often leads to situations that "we never saw coming."

Small disruptions are a natural part of organizational life, but stronger tendencies to pay attention to best cases than to worst cases often means that small anomalies don't get attention until it's too late. We argue that this doesn't have to be the case.

A final connotation of failure is that it can have moral overtones. To be alert to failures could imply that someone is to blame for the failure, not that a system is at fault or that something can be learned. Before getting caught up in these associations, keep in mind that the dictionary defines *reliability* as "what one can count on not to fail while doing what is expected of it."[31] This definition suggests three questions:

1. What do people count on?
2. What do people expect from the things they count on?
3. In what ways can the things people count on fail?

The answers to these three questions provide clues about what it is that could go wrong and what it is that you don't want to go wrong. The key word in all three questions is *what* one can count on, not *whom*. A preoccupation with failure is a preoccupation with maintaining reliable performance. And reliable performance is a system issue (a *what*), not an individual issue (a *who*). Failures are connected. Small events that are the outcome of earlier, more distant conditions predispose subsequent events to deviate from the expected.

The Mind-Set for Preoccupation with Failure

The original inspiration for this first HRO principle was a routine called the foreign object damage (FOD) walk down that was practiced on the aircraft carrier the *Carl Vinson* (CVN 70). This routine is sensitive both to cues that something is not unfolding as expected and to the fact that all systems are fallible. "Prior to every launch and recovery operation, the entire flight deck is visually inspected by the entire crew for any small loose items which may become Foreign Object Damage [now referred to as foreign object debris]. A tiny screw sucked into a powerful jet engine intake can cause disastrous results."[32] Clearly preoccupation alone is not enough. You have to report the failing, contain it, do something about it, own it, and persist if others ignore it. But notice what these imperatives accomplish. Failure now creates agency rather than fatalism. Now I can spot it and I can step in, speak up, and do something.

The tendency to normalize is with us every day. For example, recent problems with the launch of Boeing Aviation's 787 Dreamliner introduced a novel phrase, *teething problems.* This phrase was used in discussions of fires in lithium batteries, the global grounding of the 787 fleet, and seemingly similar past launches of new aircraft[33] that had problems. What remains interesting is that the cause of the battery fires was never identified, and instead, layers of defensive protections were added "to contain any future issues." The added defenses seemed to be working although a year after the grounding, Japan Airlines again reported a smoking battery on January 14, 2014.[34] In the context of managing the unexpected, to call something a teething problem is like an act of normalizing an exception. It is akin to someone saying, These are "routine fires." The result is that curiosity is curtailed, which becomes even more worrisome when the teething problem is solved, so to speak, with added defenses rather than a discovery of origins. If we are preoccupied with anything, it is the known, the successful, the simple, the confirming, and the positive.[35] Deviations are seen as an annoyance rather than news. The better HROs counteract a preoccupation with success by institutionalizing wariness. Wariness is embedded in practices that reward attention to details, detection of anomalies, familiarity with sequences, and imagination that envisions sharp-end consequences and blunt-end antecedents of anomalies. With all of this attending, detecting, and imagining, one must wonder, How does anything get done? That's the wrong question. Doing is continuous. What is discontinuous is the direction of the ongoing activity. Anomalies are the occasions of interruption when people either redirect what is being done or do not redirect the activity.[36]

It is hard to spot failing in the moment and easier to spot it after the fact. That is why a clearer expectation (recall the rationale for "concern" in the STICC protocol) often produces more information in the moment (e.g., "Should this be doing that?"). To manage the unexpected means first to put an expectation in place so that, second, departures from it become salient earlier and more vividly. In the broadest sense, any old expectation will do because it is the deviation from some comparison, the attention to detail, and the information current actions stir up that together foster reliability.

Practicing a Preoccupation with Failure

When an HRO fails, that failure can be more catastrophic than would be true in your organization. Despite this difference in magnitude, the diagnostic value of failure is similar in both settings. In either setting, failure means that there was a lapse in detection. Such a lapse could occur for at least three reasons:

1. Someone somewhere didn't anticipate what and how things could go wrong;

2. Some deviation was not caught as soon as it could have been caught; or

3. People didn't dig into unexpected events to understand their unit or system better.

All three reasons mean that the system is not as robust and mindful as it could be. This deficiency can be corrected by means of questions that probe how the system anticipates failures and actions that alter how the system handles failures and failure reporting. Questions that uncover blind spots in managing failures could include probes like these:

- What does failure mean around here? Answers often lie in small failures in the past that give clues to how the system might unravel again.
  1. What things must go right?
  2. What could go wrong?
  3. How could things go wrong?
  4. What things have gone wrong?
- Do people call attention to failures once they happen, even if others do not notice that a mistake or failure has occurred? Or do people hide mistakes and problems?
- What happens when people report concerns or failures? Are people rewarded if they spot potential trouble spots? Are they dismissed?
- Do people dig into failures to understand the system better?
- Do people update procedures if need be?
- Do leaders actively seek out bad news? Or do they simply let news come to them?
- Do people feel free to talk to superiors about problems and concerns? Do superiors listen?

If the answers to questions like these uncover areas in need of improvement, then changes such as the following may move in that direction.

Articulate Expectations

To manage the unexpected is to set forth expectations that are clear enough that deviations stand out. This is old news that comes under such headers as bandwidth, limits, standards, set point, and so on. What is different about our treatment is that we view expectations as a tool for sensemaking. Expectations provide a frame of reference. Events inside the frame remain habitual and routine. Events that edge toward the boundaries of the frame are anomalies in the making that deserve closer attention and a more active search for their story.

Create Awareness of Vulnerability

Get comfortable asking people, "What's risky around here?" Managers must sensitize employees to the possibility of unexpected errors that could escalate. People need to worry about vulnerability and feel accountable for reliability. Remember that awareness of vulnerability increases opportunities for learning. People need to be reminded that even though they think they understand their system and the ways in which it can fail, surprises are still possible. They have neither seen every possible failure mode nor imagined every possible one.

Actively Track down Bad News

Research suggests that subordinates are more likely to report good news to their superiors than bad. This pattern is strengthened when those in power dismiss bad news that threatens their prevailing views (recall the actions of senior management at WaMu). In fact, much of the discussion of safety culture boils down to the question, "What happens to bad news and to the people who voice it?" Ask that question. Don't settle for glib answers. Get others to ask that question. Sometimes people in high places dismiss surprises because they overestimate the likelihood that they would surely know about a situation if it actually were happening.[37]

Clarify What Constitutes Good News

Is no news good news or is it bad news? Don't let this remain a question. Remember, no news can mean either that things are going well or that someone is incapacitated and unable to give any news at all, which is bad news. No news is bad news. All news is good news, because it means that the system is responding. The good system talks incessantly. When it goes silent, that's unexpected, that's trouble, and that's bad news.

Consolidate Your Explanations

Seek to understand your context better. Things that are out of place in a context bear closer inspection. But be careful of the human tendency to adopt a different explanation for each small deviation. Separate, tiny explanations may hide the existence of one big problem. Gary Klein calls this kind of error a "de minimus error."[38] People commit this error when they find separate reasons not to take seriously each separate piece of evidence. What they fail to see is that one unexpected event explains them all.

This type of error is common in medical care.[39] All the symptoms point to this single disorder, but they are never combined, since each one is explained away before the next one is noticed. If key pieces of information get explained away early, they are no longer available to fill out a pattern that begins to form late in the search.

A Near Miss Is a Failure

Do you interpret a near miss as a sign that your system's safeguards are working or as a sign that the system is vulnerable? Err on the side of danger. Interpret a near miss as danger in the guise of safety rather than safety in the guise of danger.[40]

Preoccupation as Strategy

When a chief executive officer says, "Here's my strategy; here's what is important to me," translate that into "Here are errors I don't want to make! Here is where I need reliable performance!" HROs generate a deep understanding of errors they *don't* want to make. Sometimes this guideline is included under the more general heading of safety. We talk about errors you don't want to make rather than safety to heighten the demand for specificity, to capture images that are meaningful sites and surfaces, and to suggest accompaniments of strategy.

4

Principle 2: Reluctance to Simplify

"Clarification should not be confused with simplification."[1]

—David Winter

M indful organizing is a process that is sensitive to more than failures. It is also sensitive to variety and to descriptions and actions that pinpoint or hide that variety. This sensitivity, in the form of a reluctance to simplify, is reflected in comments such as these:

1. "It would be a mistake to redefine counterterrorism as a task dealing with 'catastrophic,' 'grand,' or 'super' terrorism, when in fact these labels do not represent most of the terrorism that the United States is likely to face."[2]

2. "Don't dumb down the complexity."[3]

3. "You need to treat every ski slope as if you are riding it for the first time. The avalanche doesn't care about what you got away with the last time."[4]

4. "Blaming the Ladbroke Grove train collision on operator error is an oversimplification that increases vulnerability because system screwups are left untouched."[5]

5. "We need to remain continuously aware that all of the potential modes into which the system here at the Diablo Canyon Nuclear Power station could resolve itself and fail, have not yet been experienced and have not yet been exhaustively deduced."[6]

Each of these comments, whether voiced by a practitioner or an academic, refers to a failure: a failure in the form of a terrorist attack, an uncontrolled oil well, an avalanche, a rail collision, or a runaway nuclear reactor. But each comment also reflects a more basic warning about the danger of general labels, such as catastrophic attack, a simple operation, familiar ski slope, operator error, or familiar sequences. When observers impose general labels such as these, they may neglect specific signs that the unexpected is evolving. Take former U.S. Coast Guard admiral Thad Allen's comment, "Don't dumb down the complexity." During his command of the Deepwater Horizon oil spill in the Gulf of Mexico, he kept insisting that in a complex environment, tied together by an unlimited set of interdependencies, you can't fall back on theories of simple systems. Instead, you need to pay special attention to the specific errors that are inevitable when you do simplify. Allen walked this talk through his attention to technical details and to dynamic updating of the nature of the problem, both of which helped people around him grasp continuing surprises.

Mindful organizing is generated by a *reluctance* to simplify because simplification obscures unwanted, unanticipated, unexplainable details and in doing so, increases the likelihood of unreliable performance. That's a recurring theme in this book. We have already seen this dynamic in the tension between perceptually based knowledge by acquaintance and categorically based knowledge by description. Reluctant simplification is relevant to managing the unexpected simply because categories, types, and generalizations tend to conceal incongruous details. Categories are simplifications that help us make sense,[7] but they smooth over fine-grained distinctions that may foreshadow unexpected trouble.

For example, early events in the misidentification of the West Nile virus included a tentative diagnosis that a cluster of patients admitted to intensive care had "a reaction characteristic of St. Louis Encephalitis (SLE)."[8] This was a simplification of an unusual set of symptoms, including fever, headache, mental confusion, and severe muscle weakness. Lost in this diagnosis was evidence contrary to the diagnosis. SLE is not associated with muscle weakness nor with local outbreaks only (patients localized in one area of New York City), nor does it affect birds and horses. This latter simplification is important because coincident with the human illness crows were dying in large numbers in NYC (it takes a lot to kill a crow). Although there were suggestions at the time that the animal and human fatalities might be connected, the crow deaths were not given much weight because crows don't die of SLE. That's true. But neither do humans suffering from severe muscle weakness.

The initial simplification meant that investigators forgot:

> that every other SLE outbreak in this country had begun in the south and crept up along the Ohio or Mississippi river valleys—in other words that there had always been inklings in the south before

anything happened up north. They also ignored the fact that muscle weakness—the most striking symptom in the early cases— had never been a hallmark of SLE. They didn't quickly probe the reasons for the ambiguous test results on patients' blood, and dismissed New York City officials' repeated questions about those results. Perhaps most important, they slighted the concerns of Tracey McNamara, the scientist who early on uncovered the central clues to the mystery.[9]

Useful distinctions are not necessarily rich in discriminatory detail. We tend to forget that useful distinctions are abstractions, not the things themselves, and that these things, as well as the people who observe them, are changing. Expectations are often useful distinctions that simplify the world. But they may steer observers away from the very evidence that foreshadows unexpected problems. Mindfulness, with its emphasis on context and detail, slows down the speed with which we call something "the same." And when we sense more differences, we can develop a richer and more varied picture of potential consequences, which can then suggest a richer and more varied set of precautions and early warning signs. But it's hard to complicate your categories rather than lump them into actionable simplicities, such as make or buy, friend or enemy, and profit or loss.

An especially vivid example of the problems inherent in simplification is the Columbia shuttle disaster. The disastrous simplification was NASA's mistaken judgment that the foam shedding 82 seconds into the flight was "almost in family" and a maintenance issue.[10] NASA basically simplified a 22-year his- tory of unintended, recurring foam shedding into a judgment that the puff of smoke at the base of the left wing did not affect mission success. Instead, it presumed shedding was normal and could be fixed back on the ground even though, after all these years, it still remained in the dark about why foam continued to be shed. The

Columbia Accident Investigation Board criticized NASA for its tendency to oversimplify and included a section in its final report titled "Avoiding Oversimplification."[11]

The example of the Columbia shuttle raises a broader question, namely, What does it mean to organize for reluctant simplification? We suggest that, at a minimum, it means organizing for more process variety, more openness to argumentation, and more capability and willingness to act in order to understand.

Organizing More Variety into Processes

Organizing for more process variety means to increase your repertoire of actions that register and control variations in input. Sociologist Ron Westrum argues that "a system's willingness to become aware of problems is associated with its ability to act on them."[12] This means that when people enlarge their ability to act on problems, they also enlarge the range of issues they can now notice. Another way to describe the importance of greater process variety is to see it as an increase in requisite variety. This is the idea that "only variety can destroy variety."[13]

The principle of requisite variety means essentially that if you want to cope successfully with a wide variety of inputs, you need a wide variety of sensors and responses. For example, consider the maxim "You have to fight fire with fire." In wildland firefighting, this is sometimes literally true. Conventional firefighting tools, such as using streams of water, removing surface fuels, dropping slurry from aircraft, heaping dirt on flames, or using evergreen boughs to beat out flames may be too simple to match the higher variety of fire behavior. In this case, firefighters fight complex fires with equally complex backfires in an effort to better match and manage what they face.

If people work in a varied, complex environment, those people need varied, complex sensors to register the environmental complexities. Simple expectations produce simple sensing, which misses most of what is there. Simple sensors overlook both hints of the unexpected and a wider range of options to deal with it. A loan officer who has made good and bad loans is a more complex sensor, able to sense more variety in his or her environment of clients, than is an officer who has made only good loans. A top management team whose members represent different functional backgrounds is a potentially better sensing mechanism than is a team composed wholly of finance people, attorneys, or engineers.

Researchers exploring leadership and complex systems have reworked the concept of "requisite variety" and now call it "requisite complexity"[14] to connect W. Ross Ashby's original principle to the burgeoning interest in complex adaptive systems. In part that reframing is helpful since it gives more substance to the generic word *variety*. *Variety* blurs any distinction between systems that are complicated and those that are complex. But, as complexity theorists make clear, there is a big difference between the two. A complicated system is one that can be described in terms of its individual constituents, whereas a complex system is one that can be described only in terms of the interactions among the constituents. For example, "A jumbo jet is complicated, but mayonnaise is complex."[15]

The distinction between complicated and complex may seem trivial, but consider the difference it makes in how we organize. A complicated system, distinguished by its individual constituents, is formed when people are aggregated one by one into a group, such as what occurs when positions in sales, seasonal work, and marketing are staffed one person at a time.[16] The resulting group is basically the sum of its parts, which means that this form of aggregation "draws on complexity that already exists in [individual] mental structures."[17]

Complication encourages simplification because of the necessity to create a "common operational picture"[18] among the individuals.

A different way to organize is by compilation, which both draws on existing complexity and creates emergent complexity. This occurs when, for example, two people interact and make sense of the nonobvious in ways that neither of them alone could have done. Their sense, as well as their organizing, are emergent adaptations that are more tailored to the present context and less constrained by whatever the individuals separately bring to the situation. The difference may seem subtle, but it is important. When complication is emphasized, there is a premium on matching individual expertise with the specifics of the unexpected. When complexity is emphasized, emergent interactions enact more differentiated, situation-relevant adaptations. Unexpected data can puzzle individuals and tempt them to normalize in ways that fit the odd variation into their own experience. That temptation can be weakened when the puzzle is grasped by complex interactions.

In the earliest studies of high reliability organizations (HROs), Gene Rochlin found that emerging crises on aircraft carriers were often contained by informal networks.[19] When events got outside of normal operational boundaries, knowledge-able people self-organized into ad hoc networks to provide expert problem solving. These networks had no formal status and dissolved as soon as the crisis passed. Such networks allowed for rapid interrelating, a hallmark of complexity, that increased the variety of knowledge and actions that could be brought to bear on a problem. This increased variety helped slow the pace of simplification.

Organizing for Sense-Discrediting

Organizing for reluctant simplification also means organizing for a more complex form of openness. "Real openness implies that a system is open to information that it has never thought of before. For this reason, *action* is an important informer for systems . . . If presented with the unknown, systems can be confronted with circumstances in which they need to act before they think. New experiences are therefore the source for discrediting."[20] To be open in this sense is both to believe your existing concepts and to doubt them when you act.[21]

The phrase *sense-discrediting* points to an important means to slow simplification. It is the engine that allows for simultaneous change and stability. In Michael Cohen's telling phrase, we face a "N(ever)-changing world."[22] The world we face is both like (same as) worlds we've seen before and unlike (different from) any of them. To be open in the context of n(ever) change, we need to do both what we've done before and something different from what we've done before. HROs "have to pursue simultaneous strategies of anticipation and resilience."[23] Gilbert Ryle describes this simultaneous doubt and belief in more detail:

> To be thinking what he is here and now up against, he must both
> be trying to adjust himself to just this present once-only situation
> *and* in doing this to be applying lessons already learned. There
> must be in his response a union of some Ad Hockery with some
> know-how. If he is not at once *improvising* and improvising *warily*,
> he is not engaging his somewhat trained wits in a partly fresh
> situation. It is the pitting of an acquired competence or skill against
> unprogrammed opportunity, obstacle or hazard. It is a bit like
> putting some *new* wine into *old* bottles.[24]

The emphasis in this second HRO principle is one of high-lighting structures that counteract simplification. For example, when pilots land on aircraft carriers that are moving in heavy seas, all landings are nonroutine. And yet that's not how the system handles them. People act as if the landing is both routine *and* novel. This provides both a predictable sequence of activities and an awareness that the sequence is not inviolate. The pilot remains optimistic, the deck crew pessimistic, and the system ambivalent. The system does not dumb down the complexity. As a result it is capable of a variety of actions that enable it to sense more variety during the landing. The system stays in motion and accepts the truth that it confronts a mixture of the same and the different.

Organizing for Action-Based Inquiry

Earlier we mentioned Eric-Hans Kramer's statement that "action informs systems." That insight was stated in the context of sense-discrediting, but it is also a stand-alone guide for reluctant simplification. Reluctance can be organized to reverse the tendency of early simplifications to become even simpler. We have already seen this tendency in the case of the West Nile virus, which was misidentified initially as St. Louis encephalitis. Early simplifications that ignored muscle weakness made it easier to simplify the detection and interpretation of subsequent cues.

This is the kind of scenario that is at the heart of researcher Jenny Rudolph and colleagues' exploration of the dynamics involved in "recursive interactions between interpreting and updating."[25] When confronted with a surprise, we tend to engage in "action-based inquiry" to generate more information. Specifically, "(1) problem solvers take actions and, thus, make information available for their interpretation; (2) they interpret the flow of information around them to continually reassess the plausibility of their diagnoses; and (3) they cultivate alternative diagnoses even as they pursue the leading diagnoses."[26]

Rudolph et al. use medical diagnosis as their representative example, an example that is similar to diagnosing a disease outbreak. Medical diagnosis is a context characterized by "(1) action-based inquiry—information cues become available only by taking action; (2) temporal dynamism—doing nothing or holding an erroneous diagnosis means the situation is deteriorating over time, so there is pressure on the problem solver to act on the leading diagnosis or to cultivate a new one; (3) action endogeneity—moving through the steps of a course of action changes the characteristics of the environment and the stream of cues that become available."[27] Simplification comes into play when that "stream of cues" changes and the course of action changes. Once you form a hunch of what is happening, you may put less weight on any cue that comes later. When you put less weight on subsequent cues, that lesser weight does not distinguish between cues that suggest the diagnosis is wrong and cues that suggest it's correct. A first hunch may persist, regardless of its accuracy, because subsequent cues are not given as much importance. Cues, therefore, are not inherently weak or strong. Instead, they become weakened or strengthened during processing. As people act and interpret incoming cues relative to the current diagnosis, the meaning of their current diagnosis tends to be supported, which produces less weight on subsequent cues, which increases support for the current diagnosis. A self-fulfilling interpretation is created, an interpretation that becomes further and further removed from the data.

Mind-Set for Reluctance

Earlier we said that people may neglect "specific signs that the unexpected is evolving." The crucial word here is *evolving*. We saw this back in Chapter 2, when we described how actions become mistaken. And with the present discussion of simplification, the crucial question is, How do you manage the evolving? The informal answer is, simplify as late as possible. The first simplification is the last unbiased input. Let the uncertainty build before you simplify. By doing so you may feel confused, but that basically means that you are seeing more complexity but also compiling more information. Keep asking yourself, "What's different?" When you do this, you engage in sense-discrediting. You counteract the tendency to normalize because now you are paying more attention to anomalies.[28] Sure, you're likely to be confronted with contradictions. Unsettling as that may be, it does keep your attention focused on what is happening here and now, and it makes it that much harder to mislabel something the way NASA did, as "in family."

It is also harder to simplify swiftly when there is a greater variety of interpretations. When people are more willing to speak up, there is potentially more discriminatory detail and less consensus that the situation is the same. With an increased level of argumentation, more variety is registered and can potentially be managed. With more voices, or as Paul Schulman puts it, more "partisans of neglected perspectives,"[29] you are better organized to enact a reluctance to simplify.

There is no question that requisite variety is messy. That's partly because it combines knowledge and ignorance. But that combination is not necessarily a bad thing, since it is the essence of wisdom. "The essence of wisdom . . . lies not in what is known but rather in the manner in which that knowledge is held and in how that knowledge is put to use. To be wise is not to know particular facts but to know without excessive confidence or excessive cautiousness . . . (T)o both accumulate knowledge while remaining suspicious of it, and recognizing that much remains unknown, is to be wise."[30] Thus, "The essence of wisdom is in knowing that one does not know, in the appreciation that knowledge is fallible, in the balance between knowing and doubting."[31] The more one knows, the more one realizes the extent of what one does not know. Therein lies the reluctance to simplify.

Practicing a Reluctance to Simplify

"Keep it simple, stupid" is usually welcome advice. Simple rules of thumb are easy to remember, easy to practice, and easy to teach. Contingencies, nuance, differences, and details take more effort to retain but also better register weak signs of the unexpected. When you examine the reluctance to simplify in your organization, you want to find out how the system socializes people to make fewer assumptions, notice more, and ignore less. Probes into simplifications are probes into the existence of norms that acknowledge the reality of surprise and convey messages, such as *take nothing for granted* and *don't get into something without a way out*. The following probes can help your inquiry:

- To what extent do people around here take things for granted?
- Is questioning encouraged at all levels within our organization?
- Are people encouraged to express different views of what is happening? When they do, do we label them as troublemakers?
- Are people shot down when they report information that could interrupt operations?
- Do people listen carefully to each other? Is it rare that people's views are dismissed?
- Do we appreciate skeptics around here? Do we strive to challenge the status quo?
- Do people show a great deal of respect for each other, no matter what their status or authority?
- When something unexpected happens, do people spend more time conducting an analysis of the situation rather than merely advocating for their familiar view of what happened?
- Do we develop people's interpersonal skills, regardless of their rank or position?

   If the answers to questions like these uncover areas in need of improvement, changes such as the following can trigger improvement.

Forget Some Names

A simple, ready-to-hand way to engage a reluctance to simplify is to act as if, in Paul Valery's words, "seeing is forgetting the name of the thing seen."[32] Names come automatically, as do simplifications. Treat those salient names as tentative labels for things that could be something other than what they are called. If you forget the name, then you move away from knowledge by description and closer to knowledge by acquaintance.

Think and Question out Loud

Think out loud when you raise questions about categories, propose refinements, spot limitations, and see new features of context. When you ask questions publicly this helps people understand what is going on and provides a model for them to imitate. Overt displays of thought are a good thing. Overt displays of mindful thought are an even better thing.

Develop Skeptics

Create healthy skepticism and treat skepticism as a form of redundancy. When a report is met with skepticism and a skeptic makes an independent effort to confirm or refute the report, there are now two observations where there was originally one. The second set of observations may support or refute the first set and may itself be double-checked by still another skeptic. There's no question; skeptics are sometimes a pain. But it is important to welcome them. A welcoming attitude exists only if there is strong shared sentiment that mindfulness contributes to success and bullheadedness, hubris, and self-importance do not.

Seek Requisite Variety

Skeptics create alternative frames of reference that increase requisite variety. Unfortunately, diverse views tend to be disproportionately distributed toward the bottom of the organization, which means that those most likely to catch unanticipated warning signals have the least power to persuade others that the signal should be taken seriously. Moreover, members of groups are less likely to share the unique knowledge they hold and more likely to discuss knowledge they all hold in common. That is why discussions such as adversarial reviews are so important. They discourage simplification and increase the chance of seeing a greater number of problems in the making.

Put a Premium on Interpersonal Skills

Variety has a price. The price is that it can increase the incidence of disagreement and conflict when it comes time to act. To manage this conflict, strengthen skills of conflict resolution and negotiation. Foster norms that encourage mutual respect for differences. Develop organizational agreements about how to disagree constructively, propose rules for negotiating differences, and develop policies that reconcile organizational contradictions (for example, rewarding individuals while supporting the value of collaboration and cooperation).

Revise Assessments as Evidence Changes

V. DeKeyser and David Woods show that when people get involved in unexpected events, they tend to hold on to their first interpretation even when there is new evidence that the situation has changed.[33] Fresh eyes tend to break up the mind-set that perpetuates fixation. When people resist simplification, they tend to break up fixations. Your job is to be sure that people keep updating as evidence changes.[34]

5

Principle 3: Sensitivity to Operations

"The actions made sense at the time."[1]
—Richard I. Cook and David D. Woods

The realities of unlimited interdependence get linked to limited concepts in real-time operations. These linkages do not occur simply at the bottom of the organizational pyramid, which we often call the front line. Instead, the front line we worry about, and that high reliability organizations (HROs) worry about, is located at all levels. Here are five examples of frontline operations:

1. During surgery, as unexpected bleeding occurs, the chief surgeon says to the rattled resident, "When there is bleeding

put your finger on it; don't waste time hunting for the cauterizing instrument while the bleeding continues and the patient's condition worsens."[2]

2. At the Moura mine, management paid more attention to gauges showing production than to gauges monitoring gas in the mine and the mine blew up.[3]

3. Darkness had caught two first-time day climbers on a rock face at Yosemite, and they were unprepared, upset, and off route, as they rushed to get down the rock. After several errors, which they knew how to avoid, one died after rappelling off the end of his rope.[4]

4. The Columbia Accident Investigation Board concluded that, for all of its "cutting-edge technologies, 'diving-catch' rescues and imaginative plans for the technology and the future of space exploration, NASA has shown very little understanding of the inner workings of its own organization."[5]

5. At the Diablo Canyon nuclear power plant, veteran operators counsel that you should not trust the drawings of valves and piping. Instead, walk down the whole system before you shut off the air on the nonoperating unit.[6]

In every one of these cases, we find links between unlimited interdependencies and limited concepts. Whether the concept is cauterizing, production, descending, imagining, or closing, and whether the interdependencies involve physical bodies, underground mines, moving down a rock face, monitoring a space flight, or performing maintenance, interdependencies and concepts are joined when people do something. When you do something, you change both yourself and the context around you.[7] You may realize this. You may not. The depth of this realization is what we mean by sensitivity. Sensitivity involves a mix of awareness, alertness, and action that unfolds in real time and that is anchored in the present.

When we say HROs are sensitive to operations, we mean that they are sensitive to "expectable interactions with a complicated [and] often opaque system."[8] That may sound a lot like the first two principles of reliable functioning that involve failure and simplification. But it's not. If you want to manage unexpected events, you need to put a premium on at least three processes: the detection of small failures (HRO principle 1), the differentiation of categories (HRO principle 2), and watchfulness for moment-to-moment changes in conditions (HRO principle 3). Relationships and continuous conversation are essential to all three.[9] *Preoccupation with failure* is about detecting small discrepancies anywhere. *Reluctance to simplify* is about the concepts people have at hand to do the detecting and recovery. And *sensitivity to operations* is about the work itself, about seeing what we are *actually* doing regardless of intentions, designs, and plans. The two basic reliability mandates of operations in almost any setting are (1) keep the events flowing, and (2) protect the system.[10] For example, dispatchers who control the distribution of electric power need to keep the electricity flowing but without destroying the transmission system while doing so.

In the following discussion we suggest several qualities of sensitivity to operations that affect how well you can manage the unexpected. We discuss operations as anchored in the present, as integrated maps, as heedful interrelating, as vulnerable to pressure, and as recurring issues.

Operations as an Anchoring in the Present

Operations are often described as acting in real time. Such acting is a "mix of informal, tacit, nonroutine, relational, just-in-time, quickened tempo, increased volatility, [and] informal mutual adjustments."[11] Sensitivity to operations is associated with close attention to what is going on right now, in the present. When we act, our behavior is oriented to both the future and the past but only as those exist for us at any given moment.[12] The dominance of the present moment can be tough to visualize. Suppose that you failed at some activity in the past and expect to succeed the next time you do it. Your expectation and your memory actually exist only in a brief present moment. And that momentary context, complete with its content and feelings, are what will affect your behavior. Kurt Lewin originally made this point when he said, "Only the present situation can influence present events."[13]

It is this significance of the present that lies behind our insistence that conversational sites, textual surfaces, frames of reference, perceptions, conceptual substitutions, and cultures are influential in managing the unexpected. A similar line of analysis is found in Vaughan's influential summary of research on organizational mistakes: "Individuals make the problematic nonproblematic by formulating a definition of the situation that makes sense of it in cultural terms, so that in their view their action is acceptable and non-deviant prior to an act."[14] Operations are never generated from a blank slate. Instead, definitions of the situation matter, and it is one's sensitivity to these definitions that also matters.

One way to put sensitivity to operations into practice is to be guided by the words on a sign that used to hang in a machine shop on the New York Central Railroad. The sign reads, "Be where you are with all your mind."[15] A distracted machinist with a wandering mind is a danger to himself or herself, to others in the shop, and to people who use the shop's output. Sensitivity and operations suffer when attention wavers. This was made clear when John Dill, head rock-climbing rescue ranger in Yosemite National Park, analyzed errors in judgment made before accidents that involved rock climbers.[16] He found three "states of mind," all of which represent "partial mind" rather than "all your mind." These three were ignorance, casualness, and distraction. The three, paraphrased from Dill's longer discussion, are summarized as follows.

Ignorance

There is always more to learn, and even the most conscientious climber can get into trouble if unaware of the danger ("I thought it never rained . . ."). Several partners have said of a dead friend, "I wanted to give him advice, but he always got mad when I did that. I didn't realize he was about to die."[17]

Casualness

"I just didn't take it seriously" is a common lament. It's often correct, but it's more a symptom than a cause—there may be deeper reasons for underestimating your risk. Even for experts, most accidents on El Capitan occur on the easier pitches, where their guard is down. Dill says, "With fixed anchors marking the way up and ghetto blasters echoing behind, it may be hard to realize that the potential for trouble is as high in Yosemite as anywhere. Some say the possibility of fast rescue added to their casualness."

Distraction

Dill writes, "It is caused by whatever takes your mind off your work . . . Experienced climbers were often hurt after making 'beginner errors' (their words) to get somewhere quickly. There was no emergency or panic, but their mistakes were usually short cuts on both walls and shorter climbs . . . As one put it, 'We were climbing as though we were on top.'"

To be where you are with all your mind means more than "Be where you are with all your thinking." It means that mind takes the form of thinking while acting, thinking by acting, and thinking through acting. Mind refers to a way of acting. Intelligence is "a quality of conduct which foresees consequences of existing events, and which uses what is foreseen as a plan and method of administering affairs."[18]

To grasp this way of visualizing mind and operations, we need to realize that a sensitivity to *operations* actually is more accurately specified as sensitivity to *operating* in an evolving situation. To be sensitive to operating is to view ongoing work as the "reconstituting of an evolving present."[19] Sensitivity is a mixture of agency, motion, construction, enacting, remembrance, and revision. This becomes clearer if we examine additional qualities of this third principle.

Operations as an Integrated Map

The principle of sensitivity to operations originated in observations of at least three reliability-enhancing qualities of flight deck operations on aircraft carriers. First, there were different roles in deck operations signified by crews wearing different colored shirts (e.g., yellow shirt = plane directors, white shirt = quality assurance, purple shirt = aviation fuel, and red shirt = ordnance). Second, there were frequent inspections of the entire deck for foreign object debris (FOD walk downs).[20] Third, there was a continuing broad awareness of current operations captured in the image of "having the bubble."[21]

The image of a "bubble" is a useful way to envision a sensitivity to operations. Gene Rochlin describes the phenomenon this way:

"Those who man the combat operations centers of US Navy ships use the term 'having the bubble' to indicate that they have been able to *construct* and *maintain* the cognitive *map* that allows them to integrate such diverse inputs as combat status, information sensors and remote observation, and the real-time status and performance of the various weapons and systems into a single picture of the ship's overall situation and operational status."[22] To sustain a bubble is to make an effort to assemble complex inputs into a map, a frame of reference, and a definition of the situation, in other words, a plausible story.

The idea of a "bubble" is sometimes equated with the idea of "situational awareness."[23] Situational awareness is defined as "the perception of the elements in the environment within a volume of time and space, the comprehension of their meaning and the projection of their status in the near future." We prefer the image of a bubble because it conveys a more dynamic picture of sensitivity and operations. We often hear analysts say that breakdowns in operations occur because there is a loss of situational awareness. From our perspective, we are more concerned with losing or gaining situational awareness while operating in real time. Real-time awareness drifts.[24] And when it drifts there is a better chance that we will overlook failures, settle for inaccurate simplifications, become immersed in intentions and plans, rely more heavily on preexisting routines, and comply blindly with authorities. We want to maintain the picture that Todd LaPorte creates when he describes the bubble as "the state of cognitive integration and collective mind that allows the integration of tightly coupled interactive complexity as a dynamic operational process."[25]

An example of assembling and maintaining a bubble is found in Emilie Roth's research on collective situational awareness. Roth's studies of operator decision making in simulated nuclear power plant emergencies illustrate the ways in which effective

HROs practice sensitivity to operations.[26] Operators sustained dynamic operations through a combination of shared mental representations, collective story building, multiple bubbles of varying size, situation assessing with continual updates, knowledge of physical interconnections and parameters of plant systems, and active diagnosis of the limitations of preplanned procedures. Operators were not simply aware of the situation. They built stories to see "whether actions indicated in procedure steps made sense in the context of the particular event."[27] Operators used knowledge of the assumptions and logic that underlie preplanned procedures to deal with situations not fully covered by the procedure.[28] There was an ongoing effort "to determine whether observed plant behavior was the result of known influences on the plant such as manual and automatic actions and known malfunctions, or was unexpected and signaled an unidentified plant malfunction."[29]

During the simulated operations,[30] Roth observed that efforts to improve the accuracy of representations were social and interactive: "We saw repeated cases where operators stopped to discuss as a group whether the procedure path they were following would eventually lead them to take the actions they recognized to be important for safe recovery of the plant."[31]

Operations as Heedful Interrelating

We have already seen that the ways in which people are assembled (e.g., complication and compilation) can affect group processes and outcomes. In earlier studies of aircraft carrier operations, it was found that an important contributor to their reliable functioning was what was described as collective mind. Weick and Roberts found that flight operations on carriers that had fewer serious accidents were tied together by a pattern of contributions +

representations + subordination that were enacted with care, alertness, and wariness in work teams.[32] Interrelated contributions functioned something like a mind. And the flight operations handled disturbances with more or less intelligence depending on how heedfully these three properties were interrelated. The shorthand for this pattern was "heedful interrelating."

Heedfulness is a sharpened sensitivity that involves at least three practices: contribution, representation, and subordination.

First, people see their work as a *contribution* to a system, not as a stand-alone activity. Remember that an organization is not an entity at all. Instead, it is a recurring form created by roles, rules, categories, and joint activities. When people act as if their actions contribute to the creation and functioning of something like an interrelated system, then this something begins to materialize.

Second, heedful interrelating is held together by *representations* that visualize the meshed contributions. In other words, people represent the system within which their contributions and those of others interlock to produce outcomes. In carrier deck operations, for example, safe and reliable launch and recovery of aircraft is possible only when teams are aware of the interdependencies involved in catapult-assisted takeoffs, arresting wire recoveries, and changes in the ship's course.

Third, heedful interrelating involves *subordination*. Subordination refers to the condition in which people treat the system as their dominant context, ask what it needs, and act in ways intended to meet those needs. Less heedful subordination occurs when people work to rule, partition the world into *my job* and *not my job*, act largely based on self-interest, and spend more time talking than listening.

Although heedful interrelating may sound straightforward, it is not. That's why sensitivity is so important. Jeremy Busby's analysis of reliability seeking in railroad operations makes it clear that heedfulness is tough to produce and sustain:[33] "Reliability was elusive in large organizations because people don't know each other well, don't interact frequently or intensively, have modest mutual knowledge, moved from one area or role to another, and did not collaborate over extended periods. When you can't be heedful then you fall back on propriety where 'justifiability is a necessary proxy for effectiveness.'"[34] To offset liabilities such as these, it is important to treat the five principles of managing the unexpected as a package, as we will see later in the discussion of organizational culture.

Operations as Events under Pressure

To conduct operations in real time often means that those operations occur under time pressure and production pressure. The effect of those pressures is illustrated if we take a closer look at an erroneous fingerprint analysis done by the Federal Bureau of Investigation (FBI), under intense pressures.[35]

During morning rush hour on March 11, 2004, near-simultaneous blasts hit a commuter train station in Spain's capital of Madrid, killing 191 people and injuring 2,000. In the aftermath, Interpol Washington asked a team of U.S. FBI personnel to analyze a set of latent fingerprints[36] found by Spanish police on a plastic bag of detonators left at the crime scene. Within two weeks FBI examiners had analyzed a digital photograph of the fingerprints and reported a match with a candidate print from an Integrated Automated Fingerprint Identification (IAFIS) computer search. That led to a decision in early May to arrest Brandon Mayfield, an Oregon lawyer. Two weeks after Mayfield's arrest Spanish National Police fingerprint examiners verified that the prints actually matched a different foreign terrorist. The FBI quickly released Mayfield. How did this happen?

The answers are crucial since, as we saw in the first HRO principle (preoccupation with failure), it is imperative to be clear on mistakes you do *not* want to make. In the final report of the committee that examined what went wrong in the fingerprint unit, there is this statement: "An erroneous individualization is considered the most serious error a latent print examiner can make in casework and cannot be tolerated or minimized by an agency or the forensic community."[37]

After the FBI team identified a match (and before Mayfield's arrest), they sent their findings to Spanish National Police, who had been conducting a parallel analysis. The Spanish police concluded that the match was inconclusive.[38] Later, following a face-to-face meeting with Spanish officials in Madrid, FBI personnel returned to the United States and after an all-night discussion recognized their error. A second team of FBI examiners concurred with the Spanish National Police that the latent fingerprints indeed belonged to a different suspect.[39]

The subsequent examination revealed the following sequence of operations. The initial fingerprint examination was made by a highly respected and experienced supervisory fingerprint examiner who had been selected by the Latent Print Unit chief. The examiner initially encoded *seven* identifying characteristics of the latent fingerprint, initiated a search of the automated information system (IAFIS), received a list of possible candidates from the search, compared the existing print to the candidates' prints, and identified a subject. The existing rule at the time required that a supervisor verify every latent print analysis made by an examiner that had fewer than *12* matching points. Moreover, it was routine for verifiers to know the previous examiner's results. The examiner who made the initial identification notified the unit chief, who reviewed the on-screen images and agreed that there was a match. The unit chief then assigned the case to a second verifier (a retired supervisory fingerprint examiner working as a contractor), who requested original fingerprint cards from another FBI division and after three days, also verified the original examiner's identification. "The power of the IAFIS correlation [candidate match], coupled with the inherent pressure of working an extremely high-profile case, was thought to have influenced the examiner's initial judgment and subsequent examination"[40] and led decision makers to see what they expected to see. There were problems of workload bottlenecks because the FBI examiners had too many cases to examine in the time available[41] and experienced pressure to make more identifications.[42]

We already know that pressure affects operations. But that realization needs to be built into a sensitivity to operations because pressure leads operators to fall back on first-learned, overlearned reactions.[43] In the case of the fingerprint misidentification, the role and title of *verifier* is biased toward confirmation, and it was recommended that this title be changed to *checker* and that checkers be trained and supported to speak up to people above them. Clearly it is also important for operators to be blind to the results of previous examinations. The investigation committee also concluded that the "case assignment process" should be revised. In their words, "Comparison ability should be a primary consideration, especially in high-profile cases. It must also be recognized that years on the job may not always reflect ability."[44] Fingerprint examiners routinely have heavy caseloads, but they work mostly by themselves in relative isolation. When the misidentified latent print with 7 out of 12 matching points was reexamined later by a group of examiners, they found that the initial identification was "filled with dissimilarities that were easily observed when a detailed analysis of the latent print was conducted. . . . The committee examined the latent impression and determined that it did contain sufficient ridge detail to be correctly individualized."[45] Under less pressured conditions, multiple examiners saw more.

Operations as Recurring Events

So far, it should be clear that reliability is a moving target, but the target keeps showing up day after day. Since operations are basically everyday activities, this means that threats to reliability lurk in "the crucible of the quotidian."[46] Pretentious as that phrase may sound, it is also descriptively accurate. The "quotidian" refers to events that are commonplace, everyday, and recurring, which is where efforts to make sense and hold events together operate. Calling the everyday a "crucible" clarifies that those events are a recurring test filled with interruptions and recoveries that can fan out in unintended directions. Operations that we do every day are basically a bet that things that could go wrong won't go wrong. But the actual outcome of that wager depends on how attentive we are to real-time, here-and-now activities.

Although everyday routines may blunt ongoing sensitivity, a more serious threat to reliable organizing is momentum, described as continuing in a course of action without reevaluation.[47] To overcome momentum requires that you slow or stop the action, whereas overcoming inertia requires that you start or increase an action. Momentum implies direction that continues without interruption. If you continue to engage in a failing action, this represents "dysfunctional momentum."[48] In the context of operations that are failing, interruptions could actually be beneficial if they trigger sensemaking. Sensitivity to operations need not mean that units should always prevent interruptions.[49] Instead, part of sensitivity may mean to *create* interruptions. When an interruption occurs, you have to rethink, reorganize, redirect, and adapt what you were doing.[50] An interruption of momentum, in John Dewey's wonderful phrase, turns routines inside out.[51] You see what you had been taking for granted.

The Mind-Set for Sensitivity to Operations

Operations are the site where the realities of unlimited interde-pendencies and limited concepts meet in real time. And *operating* is the medium through which these linkages are constructed and the medium through which collective mind materializes. The operating usually takes the form of continuous small adjustments that forestall larger, less comprehensible interactive complexity. When interruptions occur there is a chance to update your sense of what is actually happening since interruptions turn routines inside out. When the interruption occurs, then you have a chance to rethink, reorganize, redirect, and adapt what you were doing. Some treat the interruption as an opportunity. Most do not. Thus, part of sensitivity to operations often means that you need to exploit or create interruptions.

Operations and operating are about meaningfully staying in motion. Operators "act and diagnose iteratively in a dynamic, unfolding situation."[52] Motion and action stir up details and mean-ings that you might have previously missed. Meanings help you make sense and regain or retain some control. Implicit advice throughout this section has been not to stop the action too quickly.

Practicing a Sensitivity to Operations

HROs are hands-on organizations, all the way up through the ranks. As a result, they are in close touch with what is going on. Operations are not delegated to some while others think. Instead, HROs think *while* doing and *by* doing. That doing reflects their sensitivity to operations. Being sensitive to operations is a unique way to correct failures of foresight. A comprehensive view of current operations enables people to catch most of the smaller discrepancies that would normally go unnoticed and be left to accumulate. When you make a large number of small adjustments, there is less likelihood that any one failure will become aligned with another and interact in ways not previously anticipated. You can help your system be more sensitive to operations if you look into the extent to which people such as leaders and managers maintain continuous contact with the operating system or front line, the extent to which leaders are accessible when problematic situations develop, or the extent to which there is ongoing group interaction about actual operations. Questions that uncover blind spots in these areas include probes like these:

- Do we make it clear to everyone in our organization what we want to accomplish (the big-picture goal) and how his or her job fits into what we are trying to do?

- Do people in our organization during an average day come into sufficient contact with each other to build a clear picture of the situations they face?

- Do people in our organization readily pitch in to help out others whenever necessary?

- Do leaders of our organization pay close attention to day-to-day operations?

- During high-tempo times, or when problems occur, is someone with authority to act accessible and available to people on the front lines?

- Do people continuously look for feedback about things that aren't going right?

- Are people familiar with operations beyond their own specialty? Do people have a sense of how their work is connected with operations upstream or downstream from them?

- Do we continuously monitor workloads to determine needs for additional resources?

- Do people have access to resources if unexpected surprises crop up?

If the answers to questions like those above uncover areas in need of improvement, changes such as the following can help.

Be Guided by Actionable Questions

There are questions that focus attention in real time. We have already seen this protocol in the earlier discussion of situation, task, intent, concerns, and calibrate (STICC). A second protocol is to ask yourself three questions: To what is my attention directed (object)? With what is my attention directed (resources)? For what is my attention being directed (goal)?[53] To spell out your current circumstance in terms of "to what," "for what," and "with what" increases the visibility and context of that experience. A third protocol is one astronaut Jim Wetherbee uses. When he does an operations overview, he asks three questions: (1) Do you have a plan, (2) Is it working, and (3) Are you ahead or behind?

Cultivate Situated Humility[54]

Remember that each situation is a little bit different from the one you experienced yesterday. Be confident in your skills but humble about your grasp of the specific situation. Even the most experienced experts cannot know how a dynamic situation will unfold. Ask yourself: How might the future differ from our expectations? How might changes or problems in one part of the business unexpectedly affect other parts? What parts of the situation *can't* we see?

Encourage People to Simulate Their Work Mentally

Ask people to think of how their actions are linked with those upstream and downstream from them, how their work can unravel, and how they might correct and cope.

Make Yourself Physically and Socially Available

Don't simplify your decision making by avoiding others. Sensitivity to operations is a powerful social means to keep up with developing situations.

Reward Contact with the Front Line

Make sure to reward managers who stay close to the operating system or the frontline activities. Managers who demonstrate ongoing attention to operations create a context where surprises are more likely to be spotted and corrected before they grow into problems.

Speak Up

Just because you see something, don't assume that someone else sees it, too. In a world of multiple realities and multiple expectations, one person's signal is another person's noise. Don't voluntarily withhold dissent. When you do, you reduce the system's ability to detect the unexpected. You also increase the likelihood of continuing on a dysfunctional course of action.[55]

Bring Unique Knowledge to the Surface

The useful outcomes of seeking diverse perspectives sometimes go unrealized. Members of groups are less likely to share unique knowledge than knowledge they hold in common. Rely on process mechanisms, such as brainstorming or the nominal group technique, that encourage people to raise questions and reveal information that is not widely shared.[56]

6

Principle 4: Commitment to Resilience

"It takes a lot of knowledge to run a complex system and even more when the system is surprised."[1]

—Chris C. Demchak

Most systems try to anticipate trouble spots, but the higher reliability systems also pay close attention to their capability to investigate, learn, and act *without* knowing in advance what they will be called to act upon.[2] Reliable systems spend time improving their capacity to do a quick study, to develop swift trust, to engage in just-in-time learning, to imagine detailed next steps, and to recombine fragments of potentially relevant past experience. The signature of a high reliability organization

(HRO) is not that it is error-free, but that errors don't disable it.[3] Here is a sampling of resilience in action.

1. An aircraft is landing too low to make it to the runway, the pilot asks the engineer for "takeoff power" so that the plane can go around and try again, the engineer hears the request as "take off power," so he reduces power, and the aircraft crashes.[4]

2. In wildland firefighting, crews plan for resilience when they practice LCES. They keep track of danger by means of Lookouts and Communication, and when danger threatens they follow one of two Escape routes and gather in a Safety zone.[5]

3. Maritime organizations are accustomed to resilience because most of their operations consist of blue-water cruising away from land, rescuers, spare parts, and expert diagnoses. If a rudder breaks, if the power goes off, the crew is dependent on its own resourcefulness to do something right now.[6]

4. Recent data "suggest that passenger mortality risk on major airlines that suffered nonfatal accidents is lower than that on airlines that have been accident-free."[7]

5. You lose options if you hand over an active wildland fire to a new crew in the heat of the day rather than hand over an inactive fire in the cool of midnight.[8]

Even though these examples are varied, they share some qualities that are suggested by attempts to define resilience. Consider these three definitions.

1. "The capability of a system to *maintain* its functions and structures in the face of internal and external change and to degrade gracefully when it must."[9]

2. "The amount of change a system can undergo (its capacity to absorb disturbance) and *remain* within the same regimen—essentially retaining the same function, structure, and feedback."[10]

3. "A resilient system is able effectively to adjust its functioning prior to, during, or following changes and disturbances, so that it can *continue* to perform as required after a disruption or a major mishap, and in the presence of continuous stresses."[11]

When we reexamine the initial examples of safety zones in firefighting, breakdowns at sea, experience with recovering, good seamanship, and handoffs during turbulent change, using definitions such as these three, we find recurring themes. Each of the five examples includes adaptation to disturbances, maintenance of some functions and structures, continuing operation in degraded form, an increase in capability, and systems as the target of resilience. A commitment to act in these ways is a commitment to improve both one's generalized capacity to learn and one's ability to act during disturbances to mitigate them without losing adaptability.[12]

Anticipation and Resilience

If you take a close look at the phrase *managing the unexpected*, you will notice that the word *unexpected* refers to something that has already happened. When you manage the unexpected, you're always playing catch-up. You face something that has happened that you did not anticipate.

Think about the problems of trying to anticipate a disease outbreak, such as the West Nile virus. Robin Henig states that "there is no good way to anticipate the next disease outbreak short of waiting for a few people to get sick."[13] What is the next acquired immunodeficiency syndrome (AIDS)? You can't do much until the first wave of human infection occurs. If you find a new virus, you don't know whether it is significant until a human episode occurs. The trouble is that by the time you do establish that it is significant, the virus has already settled in. Edwin Kilbourne, a virologist at the Mount Sinai School of Medicine, describes the reactive quality of diagnosis: "I think in a sense we have to be prepared to do what the Centers for Disease Control does so very well, and that is *put out fire*. . . . It's not intellectually very satisfying to wait to react to a situation, but I think there's only so much preliminary planning you can do. I think the preliminary planning has to focus on what you do when the emergency happens: Is your fire company well drilled? Are they ready to act, or are they sitting around the station house for months?"[14]

Notice that in the reactive world of the unexpected, the ability to make sense of an emerging pattern is just as important as is anticipation and planning. And the ability to cope with the unexpected requires a different mind-set than to anticipate its occurrence. The mind-set for anticipation is one that favors precise identification of possible difficulties so that specific remedies can be designed. A commitment to resilience is quite different. Resilience is a combination of keeping errors small, of improvising work-arounds that keep the system functioning, and of absorbing change while persisting. This combination is dramatically visible in the extended example of resilience in the crash landing of United Airlines Flight 232 that we will examine shortly.

Elasticity and Recovery

Resilience is often equated with flexibility, but we need to remember that an episode of resilience requires two things. First, there has to be something that stretches without breaking. This is the property of elasticity. Second, whatever has been stretched then recovers some shape and does so quickly or slowly. Elasticity and recovery are interwoven. For example, with age blood vessels lose their elasticity and their ability to stretch without breaking. They also lose their ability to recover their former shape and to do so swiftly. A different, and slightly unexpected, example is the original meaning of the concept of "resistance to change."[15] Kurt Lewin viewed resistance to change as a property of systems. His example was continuous production on an assembly line despite the replacement of workers. He called this "the resistance to change of the rate of production." Resistance to change in this context is an achievement; it is resilience writ small. Resilience in the form of resistance should not be confused with constancy, which is explained by the simple law "The *same* conditions lead to the same effect."[16] In moments of resilience, conditions *vary* yet the effect remains the same. That difference lies at the heart of a commitment to resilience.

Recovery is often described as adapting to a surprise by reworking whatever is at hand. This is the process of improvising.[17] As Donald Schön put it, improvisation involves "on-the-spot surfacing, criticizing, restructuring, and testing of intuitive understandings of experienced phenomena" while the ongoing action can still make a difference.[18] Resilience is a mix of experience, ongoing action, and intuitive recombination, often based on some preexisting, minimal structure. The most obvious analogue of resilience is a jazz musician reworking a simple melody.[19] Part of the skill in improvisation is the ability to paraphrase, elaborate, or embellish a simple structure. Generalized to everyday life, a simple structure could be anything from a set of core values or rules of engagement to a mission statement, a credo, or a ritual. For example, practitioners in emergency medicine elaborate the simple structure ABC when they encounter an unconscious patient. They sequentially check the person's airway, breathing, and compression/circulation. The American Heart Association has recently changed that sequence to CAB, arguing that the first priority is to get the blood moving.

The juxtaposition of improvisation and resilience makes sense in the context of Ron Westrum's earlier argument that "A system's willingness to become aware of problems is associated with its ability to act on them."[20] Greater skill at improvisation is a way to increase one's commitment to resilience and to act on a greater variety of surprises. If a limited action repertoire limits perception, then increased skill at improvisation enlarges the potential actions available in one's repertoire, which should broaden the range of cues that you can afford to notice and handle. For example, medication errors were reduced 66 percent when a pharmacist was added to a team of doctors and nurses making rounds in an intensive care unit.[21] By expanding its repertoire of capabilities, the medical team was able to notice more mistakes and correct them before they became catastrophes.

Resilience in the Air Traffic System: United Airlines 232

Aaron Wildavsky clearly stated the argument for a commitment to resilience: "The mode of resilience is based on the assumption that unexpected trouble is ubiquitous and unpredictable; and thus accurate advance information on how to get out of it is in short supply. To learn from error (as opposed to avoiding error altogether) and to implement that learning through fast negative feedback, which *dampens oscillations*, are at the forefront of operating resiliently."[22]

Several qualities of resilience become clearer if we examine a specific complex system that is surprised and resiliently makes do with what remains. Just such an incident occurred when the crew of United Airlines (UA) Flight 232 on July 19, 1989, flew a DC-10 with no hydraulic systems from 37,000 feet to a crash landing at Sioux City, Iowa, 45 minutes later. When the number 2 engine, embedded in the tail, exploded, the shrapnel from the fan blades severed and drained all three hydraulic systems, an event that had never been envisioned. The result, as captain Al Haynes described it, "left us at 37,000 feet with no ailerons to control roll, no rudders to co-ordinate a turn, no elevators to control pitch, no leading edge devices to help us slow down, no trailing edge flaps to be used in landing, no spoilers on the wings to slow us down in flight or help braking on the ground, no nosewheel steering and no brakes. That did not leave us a great deal to work with."[23]

The aircraft banked sharply to the right, reaching 38 degrees of bank 14 seconds after the explosion. First officer Bill Records pulled back on the yoke and turned it hard to the left but nothing happened. The aircraft continued to spiral right. In the most important move of the incident, Captain Haynes grabbed the throttle controlling the left engine (number 1 engine) and closed it and pushed the throttle controlling the right engine (engine 3) to full power.[24] The aircraft, which would have spiraled into a crash, slowly moved to a level position. The crew immediately began following the checklist for a failed engine only to discover that none of the flying surfaces would respond. For example, in a literal confirmation of Wildavsky's description of resilience as "dampening oscillations," oscillations became one of the problems after the explosion. Roughly every 60 seconds, the nose of the DC-10 would drop as much as 200 feet, and then as the plane picked up speed, it would pitch up as much as 300 feet, then drop again (this is known as a phugoid motion, which intact hydraulic systems normally dampen).[25] These phugoids went on for 41 minutes.[26]

What this boils down to, then, is that the crew had to keep the aircraft right side up, reduce the up-and-down oscillations, and fly to an airport they had yet to spot using only differential thrusts from the two remaining wing-mounted engines. The crew, with the assistance of an onboard check airman,[27] Dennis Fitch, miraculously got the aircraft to the threshold of the Sioux City airport by means of ongoing resilient action. As Haynes put it, "We got the plane on the ground, we didn't land it."[28] The reason he refused to call it a "landing" was that the normal landing speed for a DC-10 is 140 knots, but UA 232 was accelerating at a rate that exceeded 215 knots; normal flight descent rate is 200–300 feet per minute, but UA 232 was descending at a speed of 1,850 feet per minute; and normal landings follow a straight line, but UA 232 was veering right and left because of tailwinds for which pilots could not compensate.[29]

Many readers have seen video of the landing,[30] which looks normal until a wing tilts upward sharply and escaping fuel explodes. But that video is deceiving.[31] The aircraft actually was nosing down because of the start of another phugoid cycle, it had started to tilt right at 300 feet above the ground, the crew tried to pull out of the right bank by adding power, but the left engine spooled up faster than the right engine and made the sharp tilt to the right even worse. In Haynes's words, "We just ran out of altitude trying to correct it."

When they hit the ground with the right wing tipped down at 20 degrees, the right wing and gear gouged the runway and broke off, the aircraft flipped over on its top and broke into three fiery pieces. Of the 285 people and 11 crew on board, all of whom would have died in an uncontrollable crash, 174 passengers and 10 crew survived. There might have been as many as 35 more survivors if a fire tanker on the ground had not malfunctioned.[32] Firefighters converged on the inverted center section of the aircraft, which was starting to burn. Several passengers had lived through the crash, but they were hanging upside down by seat belts and could not get out. The first fire tender truck flooded the area of fire with foam until its supply ran out 3 minutes later, and then a second tender sprayed the area until its supply also ran out. A replenishment tanker was brought in to transfer water to the two tenders, but a mechanical failure prevented the transfer. This failure allowed the flames to increase, and as a result surviving passengers died of smoke inhalation.

What Do We Learn about Resilience from UA 232?

We learn first that ongoing resilient action can be portrayed as reconstituting the evolving present. That's what we see in UA 232. The present evolves as the aircraft becomes more and less stable, as information changes, as altitude changes, and as it continues to move in the general direction of their scheduled destination, Chicago. The phrase "evolving present" sounds a little tame, considering the intermittent chaos of the incident. The evolving on board UA 232 is discontinuous, sporadic, and permeated with swift trial and error. Portrayed in this way, we can see that the crew's actions are anything but a straightforward sequence of normal-interruption-normal. And this may be true of many more instances of resilience that we experience. There is almost no reference in the cockpit to the resumption of normal flying after the hydraulics are lost. Instead, the crew of UA 232 define themselves as being in a new, distinct situation that requires a very different mode of operating. Their resilience is embodied in making do with the few resources they have left. Even though the aircraft continues to move forward rather than spiral downward, we do not see an interruption followed by normalcy. Claude Gilbert describes what we see instead: "It still seems difficult to connect resilience to the capacity to 'make up' for downgraded situations and to start from downgraded functioning in order to find new dynamics and develop new logics."[33] Those new dynamics and logic need to be constructed as a *distinct* situation, "without referring to a normal state." A situation of no hydraulics certainly qualifies as a "downgraded situation." But it is not managed by striving to recover a normal state of full hydraulics. If the crew had done nothing but turn the yoke to the extreme left to recover from the spiral to the right, they would have crashed. Instead they constituted both a distinct, new situation and a new logic of level flight.

We learn that Captain Haynes's own reflections pinpoint crucial qualities of resilient responding. Specifically, he attributed the survivable crash to five factors: "luck, communications, preparation, execution, and cooperation."[34] Many of these factors were operating because the crew had been trained in crew resource management (CRM), a philosophy and set of practices focused on teamwork with equal concentration on cognitive processing and interpersonal skills.[35] "In a nutshell, CRM training is designed to produce team members who consistently use sound judgment, make quality decisions, and access all required resources under stressful conditions in a time-constrained environment."[36] The emphasis in CRM is on identifying and accessing all available resources and managing them to deal with the unexpected. For example, while flying UA 232 the captain and first officer had difficulty making small, independent adjustments of engine speed because they had to reach around the middle throttle lever to move throttles 1 and 3. When passenger Dennis Fitch, a check airman, moved onto the flight deck, he was not of immediate help. Fitch entered the cockpit 15 minutes after the explosion, which meant that the crew was already 15 minutes ahead of him in learning what worked and what didn't. Fitch repeated most of the diagnoses that had already been made and then asked simply, "How can I help?"[37] Fitch was asked to work the throttles. He did but with an additional resource: He watched what the pilots did instinctively with their hands on the now useless yoke and matched their movements with appropriate changes in the throttles.[38] This coordination is even more striking since Haynes never once looked up at the man who worked the throttles: "I haven't the foggiest idea what the man looked like,"[39] which made for a minor embarrassment in the hospital because Haynes did not know whom to look for to thank for his assistance.

On paper, CRM training covers crucial aspects of resilience, including the topics of situational awareness, group dynamics, effective communications, risk management, decision making, workload management, stress awareness and management, mission planning, and physiology and human performance.[40] Although CRM training incorporates much that is presumed in a commitment to resilience, the two are not interchangeable. Mindful organizing suggests a slightly different emphasis on what was involved in the ongoing resilience of UA 232. All five principles were operative after the engine explosion. *Failure*: The crew is preoccupied with what failed, what didn't fail, and what is currently failing. *Simplification*: The crew abandons the simpler diagnosis of a failed engine, looks for a more complex diagnosis, and asks its maintenance base for help. *Operations*: The throttles are all they have, they can descend only by circling to the right, and they prepare the passengers for ditching. *Resilience*: They are better off with another pair of hands as they search for a flat space so that some people may survive. *Expertise*: they have 103 years of flying experience in the cockpit so they defer to the team.

Perhaps an even more important process that was operating involved sensemaking. The crew of UA 232 kept revising their explanation of what is happening and what is next. No one ever accurately diagnosed the problem as the descent continued. The crew urgently contacted their maintenance headquarters in San Francisco, but those experts never believed that the crew had lost all hydraulics.[41] Efforts to convince the headquarters otherwise were futile, and the crew stopped talking to them. Furthermore, there was nothing in the flight manuals about what to do when all hydraulics failed.

The phrase "reconstituting an evolving present," introduced earlier, is an appropriate summary of how the situation of UA 232 unfolded. We can refine that phrase with the further description that Haynes is effective because he is "recalibrating his expectations" in real time.[42] Here is what his recalibrating sounds like: "I can't reach Chicago." "If we get it on the flat ground we could expect survivors." "Don't direct me to fly over Sioux City to get to the airport."[43]

Back in Chapter 2 we described sensemaking as a process of social construction that created a workable level of certainty[44] and that "imposed order on our perceptions, experiences, and expectations."[45] That is what occurred in the air system (e.g., the superb air traffic controller in Sioux City) that developed around UA 232. But, it is not enough to call this simply situational awareness. Here is how Haynes describes the evolving experience. As you can hear on the cockpit voice recorder, there was a lot of "what do you want to do, I don't know, and let's try this, and you think that'll work, beats me, and that's about the way it went, really."[46] Sensemaking involves the ongoing retrospective development of plausible images that rationalize what people are doing and experiencing. And this capability is important in resilience. As Gilbert argues, the real disaster occurs when you lose the capacity to represent the event and to account for what is happening.[47]

The crew never lost this capacity. There was swift learning as the crew discovered what the effects were of differential applications of power and how they could use power alone to gain modest control over their flight path. Learnings were verbalized instantly and checked for plausibility and validity. They built repertoire on the spot. And that's the core of resilient sensemaking. Sensemaking is about thinking while acting. It is about implementing the recipe "How can I know what I think until I see what I say?" Or, as in the case of UA 232, How can we know what we're flying until we see how it reacts?

A little sense, a little direction, is all people need to engage in sensemaking. That minimal structure gives them a frame within which to interpret a flow of experience. And their initial actions dig up further cues that help them orient within that frame. Sensemaking is about updating plausible stories, often by means of action, while looking for data that question initial hunches.

Throughout this incident we are reminded that we should never underestimate the importance of developing a richer repertoire of abilities as a resource. "We had 103 years of flying experience there in the cockpit . . . not one minute of it under these conditions . . . So why should I (Haynes) know more. . . . ?"[48] Much of this experience had been in three-engine aircraft. That enabled the crew to recombine their knowledge in novel ways to guide a falling DC-10 to a small strip of concrete surrounded by Iowa cornfields. The loss of all hydraulics while in flight was calculated to be a one-in-a-billion chance. Subsequent attempts to fly a simulator under these identical conditions all ended in a loss of control and fatal crash.

Finally, we learn that context is a crucial factor in resilient action. This is clearly evident in Haynes's insistence that *luck* played a role in UA 232's resilience. Luck, as Haynes saw it, included clear weather with no storms; flying over flat land rather than water; a check airman on board as a passenger; hospitals in Sioux City were changing shifts and both outgoing and incoming personnel were available to treat survivors; 285 Air National Guard personnel were already at the airport for their once-a-month training session when UA 232 crashed;[49] Sioux City emergency resources had held a field simulation two years earlier

(1987) of an event that was surprisingly similar to Flight 232's crash.[50] Emergency responders in the 1987 field simulation were confronted with the crash of a wide-body aircraft, on the same closed runway 22 UA 232 used, with 150 survivors (184 survived the UA 232 crash). Behind that "luck" is considerable preparedness. As Haynes said, "We're never ready for a disaster, but you might be prepared."[51]

Mind-Set for Commitment to Resilience

HROs overcome error when independent people with varied experience interdependently generate and apply a richer set of resources to a disturbance swiftly and under the guidance of negative feedback. This is fast real-time learning that allows people to cope with an unfolding surprise in ways that are not specified in advance. This learning is anything but smooth and straightforward. Remember, the learning is triggered by a lapse in reliability. A lapse in reliability is described by the word *problematic*, which is a word that actually means the opposite of reliability. "Problematic is especially applicable to things whose existence, meaning, fulfillment, realization is very uncertain, sometimes so uncertain that the probabilities of truth and of falsehood, or of success and of failure, or the like, are nearly equal."[52]

The crew of UA 232, and many other teams that attempt a recovery, are not dealing with *probable* next steps built from logic, principles, and macro designs. Instead, they are dealing with possibilities. "In a contingent world, real-time improvising in the face of what people cannot fully anticipate [is necessary because] having designs that work as planned is only one of the many contingencies we prepare for."[53]

Resilience is about the relationship between adaptation and adaptability. In the name of efficiency, adaptation, consisting of the cost-effective use of current resources, strips away resources that currently seem useless but could prove valuable in an altered context. A commitment to resilience is a counterweight to a trap in which adaptation precludes adaptability. That trap means you're organized to deal with what you've dealt with before but not for the next surprise that overwhelms you. UA 232 avoided that trap. And a commitment to resilience is a means to avoid that trap.

Resilience is mobilized only if you're honest about your own limits. There still were 118 fatalities in the Sioux City crash. Resilience is not a panacea. It is a balancing process and that balance is dynamic. UA 232 was a one-in-a-billion event with what sounds like a one-in-a-billion recovery. The crew's landing at Sioux City could not be repeated in a simulator. But the crew's practices of staying in motion, recalibrating expectations, making sense of evolving uncertainties, and learning in real time can be repeated. And on a scale much closer to everyday life.

Practicing a Commitment to Resilience

Life in HROs is a constant diet of interruptions and recoveries. Interruption is about stretching without breaking. Recovering is about bouncing back from the stretch to something like what you started with. Resilience is important to both stages. Changes that improve resilience may look inefficient at the time. This means that your job is to encourage such so-called inefficiencies, protect the people who produce them, and frame these inefficiencies as investments in resilience. Resilience is achieved through an extensive action repertoire and skills at improvising. Probes into your organization's commitment to resilience are probes into learning, knowledge, and capability development. Those probes include questions such as the following:

- Do we encourage challenging "stretch" assignments?
- Is our company concerned with building the competence and the response repertoires of our people?
- Do we continuously devote resources to developing, training, and retraining people in general ways and in their areas of specific expertise? When there is pressure to cut costs, are funds for development and training the first to go?
- Are people able to rely on others?
- Are we known for our ability to use knowledge in novel ways?
- Do people across the company have a number of informal contacts that they can sometimes use to solve problems?
- Do people learn from their mistakes?
- Overall, can we say that most people have more than enough training and experience for the kind of work they have to do?

If the answers to questions like those above uncover areas in need of improvement, changes such as the following can trigger improvement.

Adopt a Mind-Set of Cure Rather Than Prevention

Encourage people to be attentive to knowledge and resources that relieve, lighten, moderate, reduce, and decrease surprises. With a mind-set of cure people are willing to begin treating an anomaly even before they have made a full diagnosis. They do so in the belief that this action will enable them to gain experience and a clearer picture of what they are treating. Unlike anticipation, which encourages people to think and then act, resilience encourages people to act while thinking or to act to think more clearly.

Enlarge Competencies and Response Repertoires

Resilience takes broad and deep knowledge. Generalized training and learning that increase people's response repertoires enlarge the range of issues that they notice and can deal with. So, too, does a bad day when things go wrong. A bad day uncovers new details, evokes unpracticed responses, and provides a quiet lesson in the importance of persistence. All of these outcomes enlarge capabilities. Almost any growth in your group is a small win in the sense that it increases resilience.

Don't Overdo Lean Ideals

Lean production can be a laudable goal.[54] A lean production organization works to minimize waste by focusing all of its resources on producing the best possible value for customers at the least cost. But, the lean organization can lose resilience when managers eliminate seemingly redundant positions because they also eliminate experience and expertise. This shrinks the repertoire of responses available to the organization.

Accelerate Feedback

Effective resilience requires quick, accurate feedback so that the initial effects of attempted improvisations can be detected quickly and the action altered or abandoned if the effects are making things worse. Systems with slow feedback endanger resilience.

Treat Your Past Experience with Ambivalence

The disruptions that create the unexpected are partly novel and partly routine. You've seen lots of messes, but you've never seen quite this specific mess. This means that your past experience is both partly relevant and partly irrelevant. Begin to contain the event by doing what experience tells you to do, but remain in doubt that you're doing exactly the right thing. Watch for what you have not seen before and deal with it immediately, but don't abandon your view of your past experience because that helps keep the intervention meaningful. You're attempting to engage in simultaneous belief and doubt, admittedly a difficult exercise. Your goal is to act simultaneously as though the unexpected situation you face is just like every other situation you've faced and like no other situation you've ever faced.

CHAPTER

7

Principle 5: Deference to Expertise

"What do snake oil salesmen, TV evangelists, chicken sexers, small motor mechanics, geologists, radiologists, and computer scientists all have in common? They all meet the minimum criterion of expertise, namely they all have a constituency that perceives them to be experts."[1]
—Neil M. Agnew, Kenneth M. Ford, and Patrick J. Hayes

People who are surprised when something unexpected happens manage their way back toward an expected flow of events, or they reach out to people who can help them manage their way back. In this section we suggest some of the ways in which expertise is expressed in the context of the unexpected.

First, however, we sample a handful of settings that prime our thinking about deference and expertise.

1. After the Union Pacific Railroad (UP) acquired the Southern Pacific Railroad (SP), it ignored the superior knowledge of SP crews, who knew how to work the Englewood Yard in Texas so that railcars had room to move in and out of the yard. The third day after UP had acquired the yard, it locked it up, no cars could move in or out, and this local choke point soon gridlocked most rail operations in the Southwest.[2]

2. In their analysis of the Columbia shuttle explosion over Texas, the Columbia Accident Investigation Board (CAIB) concluded that "In highly uncertain circumstances, when lives were immediately at risk, management failed to *defer* to its engineers and failed to recognize that different data standards—qualitative, subjective, and intuitive—and different processes—democratic rather than protocol and chain of command—were more appropriate."[3] The board advised the National Aeronautics and Space Administration (NASA) "to *restore deference* to technical experts, empower engineers to get resources they need, and allow safety concerns to be freely aired."[4]

3. *Chaos* is shorthand for "chief has arrived on scene." First responders size up and attack the fire. When the chief arrives the first responders defer to his or her authority, but that authority might not be matched by expertise to deal with the local situation.[5]

4. On April 15, 1989, 96 Liverpool soccer fans died when they were crushed behind steel fences at Sheffield's Hillsborough Stadium. Many died from asphyxia where they stood. The Right Honorable Lord Justice Taylor led the subsequent inquiry. Paragraph 279 in his report reads as follows: "In all,

some 65 police officers gave oral evidence at the Inquiry. Sadly I must report that for the most part the quality of their evidence was in inverse proportion to their rank."[6]

5. The first wildfire smoke jumper who parachutes out of an aircraft circling a wildfire becomes the jumper in charge. But at the South Canyon fire, this person had less experience leading a crew than did others who followed him down. Deference was built into the routine they followed. When this fire exploded, 14 people lost their lives.[7]

As we see here, expertise and its deployment can be treacherous. Expertise can be ignored by an acquiring firm, dismissed because of its presumed logic, conditioned by rank, minimized because of self-interest, or rendered secondary by prevailing routines. These are just a few of the organizational traps that can derail efforts to link expertise with the unexpected.

Reliable systems organize so that problems attract and create their own hierarchies that often propose unanticipated solutions. This practice of reorganizing around problems has been variously described as self-organizing networks,[8] migrating decisions,[9] underspecification of structure,[10] and deference to expertise.[11] The most recent phrase, "deference to expertise," alerts us both to the complexity of this seemingly straightforward practice and to the constraints that shape it.

Background

As mentioned earlier, the initial prod to examine how high reliability organizations (HROs) organize around expertise was an observation Gene Rochlin made that informal networks often resolve emerging crises on aircraft carriers.[12] Karlene Roberts, Susanne Stout, and Jennifer Halpern summarized Rochlin's pattern with an image that has become one of the most cited properties of HROs: migrating decisions. The idea of migration, first developed to make sense of flight operations on carriers, is described this way: "Decisions are pushed down to the lowest levels in the carriers as a result of the need for quick decision making. Men who can immediately sense the potential problem can indeed make a quick decision to alleviate the problem or effectively decouple some of the technology, reducing the consequences of errors in decision making. . . . Decisions migrate around these organizations in search of a person [*or team*] who has specific knowledge of the event."[13]

We later reasoned that, if you want decisions to migrate to experts, then you need to loosen the rigid hierarchy, know where the experts are, and have mechanisms to get to them.[14] These seemed to be issues of structure, and we portrayed them as the property of "underspecification of structure." Further study made it clearer that this pattern of migrating decisions was not just a function of flexible structures. Instead, it was a more complex mixture of culture, structure, perception, and action. The idea of "underspecification" was too static and failed to preserve the process by which problems moved in the direction of potential solutions and problem solvers. The process became clearer when we conceptualized migration as the practice of deference during which potential solutions emerged out of social arrangements. Furthermore, it was not so much weak structures but stronger cultures that were associated with more mindful recruitment of expertise. This loosening of hierarchical constraints represents a collective cultural belief that the necessary capabilities lie somewhere in the system and that migrating problems will find them. In other words, orderliness in the managing of expertise during an unexpected event took the form of a recurring social action pattern[15] that we label "deference to expertise" rather than a formalized chain of command.

Properties of Deference to Expertise

Readers should be careful not to confuse deference with submission. Wisdom and expertise are present in *both* the person doing the deferring and the person being deferred to. They differ mainly in relative expertise, sensitivity to context, and domain-specific knowledge, but not in giving in to the other. Deference to expertise includes a pattern of respectful yielding, domain-specific knowledge, compressed and generalizable experience, and relative expertise described as follows.

Yielding involves at least two parties (constituency and expert), which means that principle 5 is relational rather than solitary. As Sidney Dekker puts it, expertise emerges "from people querying each other, supplying data, opinions, and other input to conversations in which it can be rejected, deferred to, modified, delayed, and more. Expertise, in other words, is a co-production."[16] We are already in complicated terrain because "expertise in itself seems to be relative to the performance criteria applied in a particular context."[17] Thus, TV evangelists and computer scientists share common features. The commonality is that there is an expert interaction: "Somebody provides an explanation to someone else who asked for it."[18]

The yielding is *respectful* because participants in HROs know the limits of their own knowledge and experience. They seldom "mistake the change of a feeling of doubt into a feeling of assurance as knowledge."[19] On the one hand experts know what they don't know. They know the gaps in their own knowledge.[20] Novices, on the other hand, "have little idea of what is even included in the particular knowledge domain." This means that deference is triggered in a context of relative expertise.

Domain-specific knowledge refers to firsthand and simulated experience[21] rather than to book knowledge. That may not rule out much, but it does highlight that the expertise for reliable functioning is not pervasive. Nevertheless, it is difficult to put boundaries around a domain when it shifts depending on conditions, constituency, context, and relative experience. A rough idea of what constitutes a domain is that it is "a confluence of general information-processing capabilities, knowledge depth and organization, and environmental opportunity."[22] The important implication of the phrase *domain-specific* is that it preserves one of the more durable findings in research on experts; namely, there is "*little* transfer from high level proficiency in one domain to proficiency in other domains—even when the domains seem, intuitively, very similar."[23]

The phrase *compressed experience* is important because it demystifies expertise. Researcher Harald Mieg argues that "the core of the expert's role consists of providing experience-based knowledge that we could attain ourselves if we had enough time to make the necessary experience."[24] For example, Sutcliffe, who lived in Unalaska, Alaska, for several years, is an expert on Dutch Harbor relative to Weick, who has never been there. If Weick asks Sutcliffe, "What goes on in Dutch Harbor?" she can generate a lengthy answer based on her more extensive local experience. But, had Weick invested the same amount of time and effort into living in Unalaska, he would not have to defer to Sutcliffe for an answer. This small compression retains basically the same form when it is scaled up to unexpected events that are more consequential.

Experience, a final component of deference, can be summarized in this description: "We know with what we have known."[25] The key word here is *with*. What we have known is a tool, as well as a blind spot, and this holds true for all gradations of expertise. Experience, viewed as knowing "with what we have known," has at least two implications for deference. First, it implies that some of "what we have known" includes ideas about how experts themselves function. Our implicit theories about the nature of expertise, built from our own experience (e.g., Is expertise correlated with age, are most experts arrogant, and do years spent in a domain correlate with expertise?), affect when, on what issues, and to whom we will defer. Second, "what we have known" also includes experience with specific unexpected events. Firsthand experience in a specific domain is more or less meaningful, depending on the frequency and depth of that experience. "Going through a process once is rarely sufficient. We are always in danger of thinking we've figured out the path to success—or the route to failure—from one experience, not realizing the particular set of circumstances that makes it dangerous to generalize."[26] For example, compare the performance of people who have experienced and reflected on many unexpected events in a domain with the performance of those who have had many fewer such experiences. This is partly an issue of resilience. As Sutcliffe and Vogus put it, "Resilience from a developmental perspective does not merely emerge in response to specific interruptions or jolts, but rather develops over time from *continually* handling risks, stresses, and strains."[27]

But behind this development of resilience lies a more subtle learning that is crucial when unexpected threats occur. That learning is about closure. If you experience infrequent setbacks, then you have little experience opposing and ending such events.[28] And if you are spared from the full force of collapse, failure, and disappointment, then you never learn the lesson that bad things come to an end. If you fail to learn the lessons of closure, then bad experiences, when they eventually do occur, can seem overwhelming. The feeling is one of "I can't handle this, it will never end, and I've got to escape it." For example, experienced incident commanders (ICs) agree that the first 30 minutes of a major emergency are always a mess,[29] but eventually the chaos will begin to resolve; there will be closure. Novice ICs in training have to learn this. Before this learning, a novice can experience a chaotic beginning as an event that will continue to be out of control and get worse. So the novice may take impulsive actions that make things worse. Part of the mind-set of a more experienced IC at a wildland fire sounds like this: "Look, we'll do all we can to contain this active, spreading fire. We'll try to herd it away from buildings, but it may continue to burn until the first snowstorm snuffs it out." The more experienced IC knows that the disruption of this major fire will end somehow, sometime, somewhere. Because it always has. This knowledge reduces tension, there is more clearheaded thinking, and some-times that clearer thinking helps the IC team see a place to intervene successfully before that first snow.

Taken together these components combine into organizing that mobilizes expertise around highly varied challenges. The resulting pattern of organizing differs somewhat from the early descriptions of migrating decisions in HROs. We briefly discuss four refinements that capture these differences: sensemaking, balancing, specializing, and relating.

Refinements

Sensemaking rather than decision making migrates. Here's an example of expert sensemaking:

Fire chief: The next fire I walk into, I won't know anything.

Karl Weick: That can't be true. What do you mean?

Fire chief: When I arrive on scene with that mind-set, I draw more disparate perspectives from others, I affirm uncertainty, and I get more people to own what they see and to commu-nicate it. None of us has ever been on *this* fire.

Notice where the expertise is located. It is not in a specific person. Instead, it is emergent. And it lies within the resources of the unit, not outside it. Deference to expertise in this case means deference to the process.

This fire chief intuitively is following a path of action that is sensitive to subtleties in deference Barton and Sutcliffe documented.[30] They found that "low status individuals may become overly reliant on *the experts* and abdicate their own responsibility for monitoring and contributing to the safety of the situation."[31] The seemingly puzzled chief draws in those who might otherwise abdicate responsibility. Second, and in some ways more subtle, is their finding that people often "mistake general expertise for situational knowledge."[32] Years and years of experience do not mean that the experienced so-called expert has all the necessary information to manage the current situation. Remember, with complete honesty, the chief correctly reports that he has never been on *this* fire before.

Earlier, we discussed the signature statement that a distinctive quality of HROs is that decisions migrate. The dynamics of deference, however, suggest that it is just as likely that sensemaking migrates. Look back at that earlier description of migrating decisions. The decisions move toward people "who can immediately *sense the potential problem.*"[33] Furthermore that sensing is done by people who have "*specific knowledge of the event.*"[34] When you defer to expertise, you defer to framing, labeling, and interpreting, not necessarily to decision making. You defer to storytellers. Deference seems to move toward groups that are perceived to be able to answer the question "What's the story?" The stories that matter include at least four types of information: "what is going on, what else could be going on, what has gone on, and [what] the observer expects or intends to happen."[35] Stories built on these four components may or may not result in a decision.

But whether a decision results or not, decision making presupposes sensing, knowledge, and plausible stories. And locating these sensemaking resources, which are often found on the front line, is the aim of mindful organizing. As an example, an urban fire captain is on a run to a fire in the urban-wildland interface. While talking to a rookie he learns that the rookie has spent 20 years fighting wildfires. He says to the rookie, "When we get there, stay right next to me all the time." The captain will still make the decisions, but they will be based on the sense the rookie makes of the evolving fire.

Experts are able to make sense because they pay close attention to context. Barton, Sutcliffe, and colleagues describe this as "contextualized engagement,"[36] by which they mean that action is contingent on variations in the situation. Alarm codes, such as those that occur in hospitals, are a good example. Alarm codes mean different things, depending on what else is occurring. Depending on the context in which they occur, alarms can be ignored even if they go off repeatedly, need immediate attention but only if some other alarm is going off repeatedly, and so on. More generally, the meaning of a piece of data depends on what else is going on.

Expertise Resembles the Role of Reliability Professionals

A pattern that comes close to the expertise that we have in mind is found in descriptions of "reliability professionals."[37] These descriptions come from observations of time-pressured dispatchers who run the electricity grid in California. These dispatchers were dubbed "reliability professionals" because of their competence dealing with a volatile environment of changing conditions and the options available to them in order to perform their tasks reliably. Continuing research also demonstrated that their competence included an ability to blend system and individual levels of analysis, using both formal representational knowledge and experiential knowledge. They could recognize general patterns as well as locally relevant scenarios that enabled continuing reliability.

What is appealing to us is that reliability professionals excel at pattern recognition more than at near-complete causal analysis. As Roe and Schulman put it, "the urgency of real time makes it crucial to 'read' feedback in terms of signature events that can guide the balancing of load and generation, in the absence of operators having to have full causal knowledge of the system in process."[38] Reliability-enhancing signature events can substitute for complete causal understanding of the system.

Reliability professionals blend knowledge of patterns and scenarios into modes of performance that accomplish the balancing of load and generation. Balance, in the interest of sustained reliable performance, depends on the variety of options available in the repertoire and the amount of instability present in the demand. Balance can be described as a condition where there is a high variety of options to meet demand and there is low instability in the demands themselves (any adjustments are precautionary, *just in case* something might happen). If instability increases while a high variety of options is maintained, then more of the options are exercised *just in time* to preserve balance despite more fluctuations. Now, if the system fluctuations remain high but the options to deal with them decrease, then balancing becomes much more like firefighting. To balance load and generation under these conditions, dispatchers have to respond *just for now*, an act of balancing that can soon exhaust resources. Finally, when options are reduced to just one in a context of high instability, it becomes impossible to meet all the demand simultaneously. One option is now applied sequentially to meet portions of the demand *just this way* (e.g., an intentional rolling blackout of sets of electricity consumers). Expertise in this progression from just in case to just for now means deference to resources that can increase options and reduce volatility.[39]

Although the preceding picture of expertise may seem to be domain specific to electricity transmission, there are two reasons why it has wider relevance. First, control rooms are a place where many of the features of HROs in general are visible. These more general features include "technical competence, complex activities, high performance at peak levels, search for improvements, teamwork, pressures for safety, multiple (redundant) sources of information and cross-checks, and a culture of reliability."[40] Second, deference remains an activity that is activated when there is an interruption of flow occasioned by an unexpected loss of options or an unexpected increase in system volatility. Unexpected system imbalance is a visible form of a change in reliability as well as a change in one's own grasp of the situation. WaMu lost options while it faced heightened volatility and never recovered. The B&O museum initially faced a similar imbalance but moved back toward balance when it increased options (e.g., constructed its own engine repair facility) and reduced volatility (e.g., closed the museum to visitors during reconstruction). Across a variety of HROs we find the need to balance load and generation in real time, the need to develop as well as maintain a repertoire of responses, instability as well as uncertainty, and the need to keep the flow going as well as protect the assets. The dispatcher's job is to sense the state of this balance and to seek expertise when the limits of his or her capabilities are reached. This balancing is tougher than it sounds once you introduce lags between efforts to recover and the time when those efforts begin to have a tangible effect.

Mind-Set for Deference to Expertise

To sustain performance in the face of changes in the tempo of demands, organizations striving for higher reliability shift their decision dynamics, authority structures, and functional patterns to create the potential for a flexible response to changing circumstances. A flexible response is built partly from migrating decisions, but also from strong cultures and collective beliefs that the capabilities lie somewhere in the system and that problems will find them. When people defer to expertise, they remain alert to at least two assumptions that could be wrong: first, that authority equates to expertise; second, that the higher one goes in a hierarchy, the greater the expertise.

The mind-set for assessing and implementing deference can be invoked if you think of organizations this way: "Organizations are considered resource pools that assemble human, financial, material, and other resources . . . (T)he organization involves a connected distribution of relative expertise."[41] Deference to expertise is a way of acting, not just an abstract concept. On the surface this principle seems obvious: Who wouldn't defer to an expert when he or she has a problem? Mindful organizing, however, doesn't start there. Instead, it starts with "one's own convictions about what is real and true as well as whatever beliefs and assumptions we accept from admired or powerful others."[42] In other words, when you defer, you already have convictions that narrow what you will accept from an expert. "Conviction on the part of people in the more effective HROs is built in part on 'situated humility.'"[43] It's important to be very clear on what "humility" means here. Humility does not mean a lack of confidence. Humility is about the job, not the person. "Individuals might be perfectly confident in their own skills and abilities, but still believe that *the job* is so uncertain that no matter how skilled they are no-one can be fully knowledgeable under the circumstances."[44] The job induces humility. That job is concrete, here and now, both similar to and different from what you've done before, uncertain in what will and won't work, and bigger than any one individual can comprehend. All of this is the opposite of hubris, which shuts down emergent expertise.[45]

Practicing Deference to Expertise

Probes into your organization's deference to expertise are probes into accountability, responsibility, and awareness of where to go for help. But they are also probes into your culture and its recurring patterns of social action. The following questions begin to suggest how deference to expertise is practiced in your organization.

- Do people in our organization respect the nature of one another's work?
- Do people in our organization value expertise and experience over hierarchical rank?
- If something out of the ordinary happens, do people in this organization know who has the expertise to respond?
- In our organization is it easy for us to obtain expert assistance when something comes up that we don't know how to handle?
- If something unexpected occurs here, do we involve the most highly qualified people, regardless of rank, in sensemaking and decision making?

If the answers to questions like those above uncover areas in need of improvement, changes such as the following can trigger improvement.

Ask for Help

If people in HROs get into situations they don't understand, they're not afraid to ask for help. In a macho world asking for help or admitting that you're in over your head are often frowned upon. But good HROs don't allow that to happen. It is a sign of strength and confidence to know when you've reached the limits of your knowledge and know enough to enlist outside help.

Create Flexible Decision Structures

Identify pockets of expertise before you need them. Don't assume the expertise is at the top and disappears as you go down the hierarchy. When problems occur, let decision making migrate to people who have the most expertise to deal with the problem. This means that expertise and experience are more highly valued than rank when unexpected situations arise.

Encourage Imagination as a Tool for Managing the Unexpected

"Imagination is not a gift usually associated with bureaucracies,"[46] but it is an attribute that is associated with the better HROs. Mindful management of the unexpected presumes that systems value imagination. Managing the unexpected consists partly of extrapolating the possible effects of small discrepancies, imagining scenarios not yet experienced, constructing hypothetical lines of action, and envisioning what might have been overlooked by a narrow set of expectations. These are operations of imagination that can feel alien in cultures obsessed with measurement and quantification. Spend time simulating alternative scenarios of anticipated futures,[47] and work backward from an imagined outcome to identify the events that could bring that outcome about.

Beware of the Fallacy of Centrality

You need experts if you want to cope mindfully, but you need to be sure that your experts have a realistic view of their expertise. If you defer to an expert who has limited self-awareness, you're in trouble. Here's why. Ron Westrum, observing the diagnostic practices of pediatricians in the 1940s and 1950s, spotted what he has come to call the "fallacy of centrality." The fallacy is this: Under the assumption that you are in a central position, you presume that if something serious were happening, you would know about it. And since you don't know about it, it isn't happening. It is precisely this distortion that kept pediatricians from diagnosing child abuse until the early 1960s. Their reasoning? If parents were abusing their children, I'd know about it; since I don't know about it, it isn't happening. If you commit the fallacy, then you feel no need to defer to expertise simply because nothing is happening and nothing needs to be solved.[48]

Refine Your Grasp of Expertise

When people are entrusted with dangerous technologies, it is easy for them to feel self-important and central since they live on a steady diet of people telling them that they *are* important. There is a grain of truth to these attributions. But that does not mean that these experts are also all-knowing. Possibly worse, if other people assume that you are all-knowing, then they won't take the trouble to tell you what they know since they assume that you already know it. Sometimes people who are lower in a hierarchy fail to raise questions or act on their concerns out of fear—fear of repercussions or fear of stepping on someone's toes. However, even when fear is absent, some people defer to experience because they equate it with expertise; they believe that their more experienced colleague must "know what's best."[49]

Listen with Humility

Be wary of inflating your own expertise, and be wary of others who inflate theirs. Self-important people know less than they think they do, are less curious about the world than they need to be, and are vulnerable to more surprises than they are prepared for. The mistaken claim that "nothing is happening" means simply that no one was looking, asking, or listening.

8

Organizational Culture and Reliability

"Until I came to IBM, I probably would have told you that culture was just one among several important elements in any organization's makeup and success—along with vision, strategy, marketing, financials, and the like . . . I came to see, in my time at IBM, that culture isn't just one aspect of the game—it is the game."[1]

—Lou Gerstner Jr.

"The pursuit of excellence over time became an obsession with perfection. It resulted in a stultifying culture and a spider's web of checks, approvals, and validation that slowed decision making to a crawl . . . I can understand the joke that was going around IBM in the early 1990s. 'Products aren't launched at IBM. They escape.'"[2]

—Lou Gerstner Jr.

When we talk about the five principles of mindful organizing, we sometimes refer to them individually, and sometimes we call them a "package." This chapter is more about the package than the individual principles. To talk about mindfulness as a package is to inch toward the idea of a framework, a mind-set, and a cluster of values, all of which inch us closer to the notion of organizational culture. When we talk about mindfulness and culture, we must sound a little foolish since both concepts seem to be sprawling catchalls. Culture, for example, is "a term readily recruited to explain virtually everything, including successes and failures, emotions and thoughts."[3] We don't want to add to that sprawl, but we do want to address the reality that mindfulness, despite all its breadth of meaning, is still constrained, malleable, and coordinated. And those constraints on mindfulness are embodied in culture. Those constraints influence what it means to manage the unexpected and what it means to have expectations in the first place. The goal of this chapter is to lend substance to that assertion and to illustrate the argument with a close look at peaks and valleys in reliable functioning at Toyota Motor Corporation.

What Is Organizational Culture?

Barry Turner's work in the early 1970s remains one of the clearest descriptions of culture and its importance for organizing. In Turner's words, "*Part* of the effectiveness of organizations lies in the way in which they are able to bring together large numbers of people and *imbue* them for a *sufficient* time with a *sufficient similarity* of approach, outlook and *priorities* to enable them to achieve collective, *sustained* responses which would be impossible if a group of unorganized individuals were to face the same problem. However, this very property also brings with it the dangers of a *collective blindness* to important issues, the danger that some vital factors may be left outside the bounds of organizational perception."[4]

We have italicized key words that give form to the idea of culture. To call culture "*part* of the effectiveness" is to make clear that when we argue that culture matters, that does not mean that structure, personnel composition, and strategy don't. To say that culture "imbues"[5] people is to claim that culture saturates or permeates activities, which seems closer to wishful thinking than to what actually happens. If saturation were truly successful, then there would be no need for the distinction between formal and informal culture.[6] "Sufficient" influence is a shrewd choice of description because small commitments can have lasting, broad effects. The phrase "sufficient similarity" is meaningful because the rhetoric of culture often goes overboard in suggesting how completely the outlook and priorities are shared. Shared outlooks sometimes sound like people become interchangeable in how they think and act. They're not. There is some sharing and some similarity but it is far from total.[7] "Priorities" and prioritizing are important outcomes of culture and often take the form of "gradations of relevance"[8] ranging from central to more peripheral. "Sustained" responses are those that continue despite changes in personnel. And "collective blindness," something that became much more visible through Turner's early work[9] on manmade disasters, is the main reason that culture (particularly the idea of safety culture) is prominent in most discussions of reliability. As will become clear in the discussion of Toyota's emerging blind spots, the culture that was thought to give it an advantage also led it to misinterpret customer complaints and further jeopardize quality.

The subtleties within Turner's description are made clearer by Stanford University researchers Debra Meyerson and Joanne Martin, who have argued persuasively that culture is not monolithic, nor is it defined completely by harmonious and shared meanings (this is known as an integration view of culture).[10]

When you describe culture as shared, you ignore the fact that there are also subcultures that are in conflict with one another (this is known as a differentiation view of culture) and individuals whose interpretations are irreconcilable and difficult to put boundaries around (this is known as a fragmentation view of culture). Each form of culture handles ambiguity differently: Integration denies it, differentiation selectively clarifies it, and fragmentation accepts it.[11] In a mindful culture, all three forms of culture are present.

With these foundations in mind, we want to examine a more recent definition of culture that engages more directly with sensemaking, communication, and sustained action in the face of the unexpected. Tony Watson describes culture as "The system of meanings which are shared by members of a human grouping and which define what is good and bad, right and wrong, and what are the appropriate ways for members of that group to think and behave."[12]

We see here the expected references to culture as shared meanings, as directed at behavior, as a set of coherent guidelines ("system of meanings"), and as focused on what is socially appropriate. What is distinctive is the inclusion of values. If we treat values as "core beliefs about what is important, right, good, and desirable,"[13] then these beliefs serve much the same function as do rules, but they do so with more flexibility. As we have seen, flexibility is crucial in managing the unexpected, but so, too, is structure in the form of lessons learned from previous trials and errors and a script on which to improvise (e.g., situation, task, intent, concerns, and calibrate [STICC]). Culture can provide both stability and flexibility.

The possibility that culture can simultaneously produce stability and flexibility was one of the important contributions to theory[14] that Tom Peters and Robert Waterman Jr. made in their influential book, *In Search of Excellence*.[15] *Loose-tight* was a summary phrase that stood for the idea that firms should tightly couple their employees to a small number of values that must be followed (usually no more than three) but allow discretion on everything else. This produces some centralization but it is loosened when everyday decentralized practice reaches into novel locales that require novel adaptations and recoveries. There is flexibility built on a sufficiently common mind-set. For example, Applied Energy Services (AES), a firm Waterman Jr. cofounded, was held together by a culture built of four core values (fairness, integrity, social responsibility, and fun). Employees who became tightly coupled to these values received autonomy because they would do the *right thing.* These values enabled the firm to disperse decision making throughout the company to people who were closer to the action. Top management still gave advice. But they made very few decisions since the culture enabled good sense-making and made for good judgment and good decisions.

Given this line of argument, a closer look at the content of culture and its effects would include questions such as, "To what extent are the espoused values accepted as core beliefs, how strong are the sanctions for ignoring them, and what subset of people are presumed to hold these beliefs?"[16] Furthermore, sustained, locally adaptive reliable performance suggests a history of socialization that those who see the group as exemplary may miss. When you observe "what appears to be successful decentralization, if you look more closely, you will discover that it was always preceded by a period of intense centralization where a set of core values were hammered out before the people were turned loose to their own 'independent' ways."[17]

How Culture Develops

Of the many recent descriptions that attempt to capture key properties of cultures, Edgar Schein's is perhaps the best known.

In Schein's view culture is defined by six formal properties: "(1) shared basic assumptions that *are* (2) *invented*, discovered, or developed by a given group *as it* (3) *learns* to cope with its problem of external adaptation and internal integration in *ways that* (4) *have worked* well enough to be considered valid and, therefore, (5) *can be taught* to new members of the group *as the* (6) *correct way* to perceive, think, and feel in relation to those problems."[18]

Schein's list of six properties of culture has been purposely made tougher to read because of italics that span the numbered phrases. Those italics are there for a reason, namely, to capture that culture is indeed developing, visible in transitions, and dynamic. For example, assumptions are not just shared intact; that sharing involves inventing. Culture is something learned, but more accurately it is an ongoing process of learning what works. If you think back to Turner's foundational definition, he emphasizes "sufficient" similarity, which means good enough for the time being but not necessarily permanent. Schein does make clear that when we talk about culture, we are talking about:

- Assumptions that preserve lessons learned from dealing with the outside and the inside (e.g., Don't sign anything.).
- Values derived from these assumptions that prescribe how the organization should act (e.g., Never get into something without a way out.).
- Artifacts or visible markers and activities that embody and give substance to the espoused values (e.g., Live by the laminated card in your pocket that lists our values.).
- Ways of doing business (e.g., Never hand over a fire in the heat of the day.).

Artifacts are the easiest to change, assumptions the hardest.

What Schein has spelled out in careful detail, people often summarize more compactly: Culture is "how we see and do things around here." Or, with less latitude, "We do things in a particular way around here, don't try doing things differently."[19] For our purposes, we modify those summaries slightly and argue that culture is also "what we expect around here." Cultures affect both what people expect from one another internally (these expectations are often called norms) and what people expect from their dealings with the external environment of customers, competitors, suppliers, shareholders, and other stakeholders.[20]

Notice that these internal and external expectations help us *interpret* what is going on. But these expectations also help us *express* ourselves. This twofold function of culture is captured by Stian Antonsen, who describes culture as "The frames of reference through which information, symbols, and behaviour are interpreted and [through which] the conventions for behaviour, interaction and communication are generated."[21] Culture provides a frame of reference that consolidates plausible interpretations. But it also provides a language we use to express ourselves in interaction and communication. When culture influences both interpretation and expression, it can create a self-fulfilling prophecy. For example, if, as an engineer, you expect that nonengineers know nothing (interpretation), then you won't talk to them to discover what they do know (expression). And since you have no input from nonengineers, it's easy to conclude that nonengineers know nothing and engineers know best. What you fail to see is that your own culture-driven behavior made that false prophecy come true.

Culture affects how we detect, interpret, and learn from disrupted expectations. What differs from group to group is the extent to which people agree on what is appropriate and how strongly they feel about the appropriateness of the attitude or behavior. If everyone feels strongly about the importance of a behavior, there is little latitude for deviation, and slight departures from the norm are dealt with swiftly and harshly. For instance, if a group of surgeons feels strongly that checklists "take too much time" and are for "cowards," anyone who tries to use one unobtrusively is subject to ridicule. If, however, people feel less passionate about the issue, then there is a weaker norm around checklists. And what would qualify as a deviation now is more a matter of style, technique, or preference.

As culture develops, several things have to fall into place for it to persist. Charles O'Reilly argued that a culture held together by norms of appropriate behavior will not persist unless:

- Top management conveys a clear preference in its beliefs, values, and actions.
- Those top management actions and words are communicated credibly and consistently and remain salient for everyone.
- Those communicated values are seen to be consistent rather than hypocritical and are felt strongly by the majority of people.
- Bonuses, raises, promotions, and approval flow toward those who act appropriately and away from those who don't.[22]

That list contains lots of places where leaders' efforts to build a strong, mindful culture can get sidetracked.

The Case of Toyota

To illustrate how culture can heighten mindfulness and how it can create blind spots, we use the case of Toyota. Toyota, founded in 1936, has long been recognized as one of the finest manufacturing companies the world has ever seen.[23] Given Toyota's vaunted position, it is hard to understand how such a renowned company could experience the kinds of problems that dominated the headlines during 2009–2011. When the top dog in the very mature automobile industry can falter, what does it say about sustainable performance in a world of surprises?[24] It says a lot and that is why we use Toyota to illustrate how variations in mindfulness and variations in outcome can covary.[25]

The Toyota Way

Toyota Motor Corporation (TMC) began perfecting its production system in the mid–twentieth century, drawing heavily on the work of W. Edwards Deming, the writings of Henry Ford, and personal observations by Toyota delegates who visited Ford Motor Company and other businesses in the United States in the 1950s.[26] Contrary to general impressions of the genesis of the Toyota Production System (TPS), the inspiration came from visits by Toyota personnel to a supermarket. There they saw how the supermarket only reordered and restocked goods once customers had bought them.[27] The TPS, in contrast with the prevailing mass production systems, "introduced smooth flows, low inventories, reduced variability at every stage of production, faster die changes, pull systems, and visible controls, together with empowerment of employees and strategically managed relationships with suppliers."[28] Over time Toyota's management philosophy evolved, and in April 2001 Toyota adopted the Toyota Way. Industrial engineering professor Jeffrey Liker, who has studied Toyota for decades, describes the Toyota Way as a set of 14 principles[29] that have shaped Toyota's learning-oriented culture.[30] "The more I have studied TPS and the Toyota Way, the more I understand that it is a system designed to provide the tools for people to continually improve their work. The Toyota Way means more dependence on people, not less.

It is a culture, even more than a set of efficiency and improvement techniques."[31]

The Toyota Way has two "main pillars."[32] The first pillar is the principle of "Continuous Improvement" ("*kaizen*").[33] *Kaizen* is "the process of making incremental improvements, no matter how small."[34] Toyota itself notes that "we are never satisfied with where we are and always improve our business by putting forth our best ideas and efforts."[35] The second pillar is "Respect for People."[36] According to Toyota, this includes building mutual trust and responsibility, communicating sincerely, and promoting personal and professional growth and teamwork.[37]

There is some overlap between the processes and practices that characterize high reliability organizations (HROs) and the attributes of the espoused Toyota Way. Much as HROs seek to continuously learn about potential threats to reliability, Toyota's principle of continuous improvement reflects a similar desire to learn and grow. Toyota's second pillar, respect for people, reflects ongoing efforts to ensure that employees make every effort to understand others and take responsibility to build mutual trust. HROs pursue similar goals in their efforts to remain sensitive to operations, to contain problems that arise, and to create a context of trust and respect.

Given the early parallels between the Toyota Way and HRO principles, what happened as these parallels began to dissolve into crises between 2009 and 2011? How could a company that practiced a widely admired management philosophy designed to ensure quality and continuous improvement devolve into a company characterized by neither? And then recover? We turn next to possible answers.

The Unfolding Crisis: 2009–2011

In 2007 Toyota made record global profits while its American rivals, such as General Motors and Ford, all lost money.[38] But all was not well at Toyota. Early warnings of Toyota's problems surfaced in 2007 and 2008 when Consumer Reports and J. D. Power and Associates, two influential automotive ratings agencies, noted a variety of small issues and concluded that Toyota's overall vehicle quality had measurably decreased in recent years. In September 2007 Toyota issued a recall for a Lexus part to fasten floor mats to car floors to avoid acceleration problems. In January 2008 Chris Tinto, Toyota's U.S. vice president in charge of technical and regulatory affairs, warned his fellow executives that "some of the quality issues we are experiencing are showing up in defect investigations."[39] Still most managers believed that quality control was so deeply embedded in Toyota's DNA that there couldn't be any real problems.[40]

Problems in the United States reached a turning point on August 28, 2009, when an off-duty highway patrolman called 911 from his Lexus as it sped out of control down a San Diego highway.[41] The call ended when the Lexus crashed into another vehicle and careened over a cliff. All four passengers were killed.[42] The accident ignited a surge of publicity not only because the 911 tape was publicly released but also because of the credibility and driving expertise of a highway patrol officer.[43] Between September and November 2009 Toyota issued a safety advisory on floor mats in approximately 4 million vehicles and announced a redesign to address floor mats and brakes.[44] But their problems didn't end there. Between August 2009 and August 2010 Toyota recalled nearly 10 million vehicles—a very large number given that the company had sold only about 7 million vehicles during this same period.[45] And the number of recalls kept growing. *Automotive News* reported in May 2011 that more than 20 million Toyota vehicles had been recalled since autumn 2009. Recalls concerned several issues: potentially sticky brake pedals, loose floor mats that inadvertently held down the gas pedal, and possible problems with software that controlled the engine and braking function.[46] Other quality problems included corrosion in the pickup truck frames and minor complaints of stalling in some models.[47] Regardless of the causes of these events, the highly publicized recalls called into question Toyota's reputation for safe and reliable vehicles.[48]

Toyota responded to the crisis by commissioning two panels[49] of esteemed, independent outsiders to examine its quality processes and to provide objective recommendations to the highest levels of Toyota's management. The North American Quality Advisory panel concluded that the root causes of Toyota's challenges went beyond the rapid growth that it had experienced in the decade preceding the recalls. In fact, the root causes were much more complex and were embedded in the organization's management systems, leadership, and most important, its culture.[50] The causes, like the causes of many crises, were "not unique to Toyota."[51] TMC president Akio Toyoda admitted as much in his prepared testimony before the U.S. House Committee on Oversight and Government Reform held on February 24, 2010. Toyoda told the committee that Toyota's traditional priorities of safety first, quality second, and volume third "became confused, and we were not able to stop, think and make improvement as much as we were able to before, and our basic stance to listen to customers' voices to make better products has weakened." He went on to say that "I would like to reaffirm the values of placing safety and quality the highest on our list of priorities."[52]

The Toyota Way might have enabled Toyota's success. But in its efforts to cut costs and become the top-selling automaker in the world,[53] Toyota began to overlook problems rather than digging into them. Toyota promised to be customer focused but repeatedly blamed customers' errors as the main cause of the accidents. Years of withholding information, dismissing customer complaints, and responding slowly to the problems clearly violated its founding principles of *kaizen*.

The Drift of Toyota's Mindful Culture

Toyota's unexpected crises can be partially explained by an overall weakening of the mindfulness embodied in its organizing. Through the lens of high reliability organizing, we can see in hindsight that Toyota was preoccupied with success rather than with digging into its failures. It developed blind spots that hindered its ability to recognize emerging problems and to respond appropriately. It dismissed complaints by customers and regulatory agencies. It simplified interpretation of the root causes of certain events. It failed to attend to current operations, it lost resilience, and it favored authority over expertise.

Preoccupation with Success Rather Than Failure   In an interview with Wharton professor John Paul McDuffie, Professor Takahiro Fujimoto, a leading authority on the Toyota production system and automotive development, observed that during the decade preceding Toyota's challenges, "Middle managers, particularly at headquarters, started to drift from the Toyota Way by being arrogant, overconfident, and also they started not to listen to the problems that customers raised."[54] In other words, Toyota stopped being preoccupied with failure, stopped anticipating what might go wrong and how it could go wrong, and stopped looking carefully at what had gone wrong to understand the health of its overall system better. Toyota became complacent. As Toyota president Toyoda admitted, Toyota's executives suffered from "hubris born of success."[55]

Fifty years of consecutive success in the form of profits and reputation can breed overconfidence and complacency. But there is an unexpected vulnerability in the principles of the Toyota Way. The principle that "the right process will produce the right results" contributed to a culture where employees were discouraged from listening carefully to customers' complaints due in part to a collective belief that "we know best." After all, if the right process is doing what it should be doing—in essence, producing the right results—then complaining customers must be ill informed, and the problem is their fault.[56]

Simplifying Assumptions and Interpretations Teams and networks of individuals with different perspectives are critical in organizing for higher reliability. Divergent perspectives and viewpoints help an organization resist the tendency to decide in advance which problems merit attention and which do not. Requisite variety encourages the questioning of preconceived assumptions, categories, and conclusions. It's important to avoid simplifying assumptions and interpretations, especially if the context keeps changing. But Toyota did just the opposite. Toyota assumed that its assumptions, especially those the engineering group made, were right; that it understood the context; and that customers were wrong. It reacted to customer complaints with a degree of skepticism and defensiveness. It also simplified its interpretations of customer feedback. As James Lentz, current chief executive officer (CEO) of Toyota North America, told the House Committee on Energy and Commerce in February 2010: "With respect to pedal entrapment, Toyota conducted investigations of customer complaints, which focused too narrowly on technical issues without taking full account of the way customers used our vehicles."[57] The control Toyota's engineering group exercised limited the degree to which Toyota even considered other perspectives.

Insensitivity to Operations Toyota's culture of reliability was enabled by an organizational structure that standardized many of its practices into inviolable routines. These very same practices, however, hindered the ability to monitor the larger interdependencies to keep unexpected, small problems from growing bigger.

With decision making centralized in Japan, local capabilities for collaborative, prompt problem solving were underdeveloped. Furthermore, the Union of Japanese Scientists reported a disconnect internally between Toyota's senior management and employees in divisions responsible for manufacturing, sales, and customer satisfaction. As a result senior managers were ill informed about serious issues, customer perspectives, and social expectations.[58] This meant that Toyota was slow to respond to the emerging "quality and safety issues."[59]

Lack of Resilience   The volume of Toyota's sales grew rapidly during the decade preceding the recalls. Yet the number of Toyota field personnel in overseas markets stayed basically the same. Training over this period also was inadequate. This was unfortunate because as we know, resilience comes from deep technical expertise and more generalized capabilities that enlarge response repertoires. Moreover, Toyota's hierarchical structure of global operations aimed to maximize "control by TMC in Japan."[60] For example, as the North American Quality Advisory Panel reported, lawmakers criticized Toyota for having only "one device in the U.S. that could decode crash data from event data recorders (EDRs) installed in Toyota vehicles. Neither law enforcement personnel, regulators, nor Toyota dealers could access the data in Toyota's EDRs. To many, this was another example of an attempt by TMC in Japan to maintain control—in this case, control of vehicle crash data."[61]

Toyota publicly acknowledged its shortcomings in the development of resilience and in sharing best practices and knowledge across the entire organization.[62] For example, Toyota did not connect the Lexus recall in the United Kingdom in 2000—a floor mat issue—to the floor mat issues in the United States. The sticky-pedal issue also was reported in Europe, and a recall conducted, before the sticky-pedal recalls in the United States.

Congress criticized Toyota for not recognizing more quickly that the sticky pedals were a broader issue across markets. Toyoda publicly addressed this criticism, stating that Toyota "failed to connect the dots between problems in Europe and problems in the United States."[63] A Toyota executive explained before the U.S. Congress that Toyota doesn't do a "very good job of sharing information across the globe" as the information is often one way—flowing from regional markets, such as the United States, Canada, or Europe, back to Japan.[64]

Deference to Authority Rather Than Expertise Toyota was a global organization structured to "maximize control" by its Japanese headquarters.[65] Its functions were centrally managed with no unified leadership in each region or country.[66] And this had clear effects on the interpretation of where expertise was located. When the unfolding problems occurred, information sharing and decision making did not migrate, which limited the organization's ability to understand and solve disruptions.

Deference to hierarchical rank and structure also affected the quality of Toyota's responses to problems. People located away from headquarters didn't have enough context or expertise to resolve them. One prominent example concerns the president and CEO Toyoda, who decided not to attend the U.S. congressional hearings on the automaker's safety lapses.[67] Instead Toyoda wanted to send executives working in the United States to testify on behalf of the company. In a statement to reporters, he said: "I trust that our officials in the U.S. will amply answer the questions. . . . We are sending the best people to the hearing, and I hope to back up the efforts from headquarters."[68] Toyoda agreed to appear at the hearings only after considerable congressional and public pressure.[69]

As we saw earlier Toyota's quality-engineering operations in Japan thought it knew best. And as we saw earlier, this viewpoint is

a good example of the fallacy of centrality. Engineering operations did not seek or share information about customer complaints with others internally, such as those in the field closer to
the problems. And they dismissed input and feedback from
customers.[70] As a result of this organizational structure and
mind-set, Toyota sacrificed "trusted relationships with local
customers and other stakeholders" as well as the ability "to act
quickly to identify and address the root causes of small problems
before they become large ones."[71] Centralized engineering itself
received limited input from other regions that might have had a
better understanding of issues with customers. The prevailing
attitude, Fujimoto summarized, was overconfidence expressed as
"This is none of your business." "They (Toyota) always say 'We
want to find problems. So please give us any clues on the problems
you see.' But if I actually say, 'This is a problem for you,' they say,
'This is none of your business. We have to find the problem. Not
you.' This attitude was growing for some time, I think, in some
parts of headquarters. That was very dangerous. It is a good time
to correct this kind of attitude and go back to the basics of the
Toyota system."[72]

Reorganizing at Toyota

Toyota began moving toward a more mindful culture when it
released its framework called Global Vision 2020 on March 8,
2011. The Vision signaled Toyota's recommitment to safety,
quality, constant innovation, and sustainability. It also outlined a
global framework for decentralizing and regionalizing operations.
Toyota envisioned that Toyota headquarters would provide overall
direction and support for initiatives undertaken by regional operations, but regional operations would develop their own missions
and strategies to support the vision. Regions would decide how best

to serve customers and would play a bigger role in product development and design.[73] In fact, before its announced vision change, Toyota already had begun to address challenges related to regional autonomy and balancing global versus local control.

In addition to reaffirming its central values, Toyota reorganized its organizational infrastructure and management systems. For example, Toyota restructured management by decentralizing decision-making authority and simplifying reporting structures. Specifically, it appointed North American leaders and others as presidents of plants in the United States, Canada, and Mexico. In addition, it created several new positions that were specifically concerned with safety (e.g., chief safety technology officer for the entire corporation and product safety executives for each region).[74]

Toyota established a "Voice of the Customer Database." The purpose was to make customer data more visible and to improve the flow of customer data from its dealer networks. In addition, Toyota sought to integrate data sources (both hard technical data and softer quality and safety data) and to make the information system more broadly accessible.[75]

Toyota created Swift Market Analysis Response Teams (SMART teams) in the United States to analyze and respond to customer complaints more quickly. To increase requisite variety, SMART teams were composed of both engineers and field technicians, and their job was to contact customers within 24 hours and, when necessary, to conduct on-site inspections of vehicles. And Toyota upgraded networks of technical offices to respond more quickly to reports of serious quality issues.[76]

Chapter Summary

How did the world's preeminent automotive company get into and out of such a mess? With the framework of HRO in mind, we see that Toyota's culture impeded its ability to make sense of and respond appropriately to the challenges it faced. Toyota had in place processes for continuous improvement and an organizational culture that valued these processes. However, it focused these efforts rather narrowly on internal engineering, design, and production operations, instead of applying them more broadly to the entire organization, including sales and customer service. In the face of rapid changes, complex issues, and competing sources of information, this narrow focus turned problematic. Toyota was not aware that its existing practices were missing signals of trouble. As a result, Toyota developed blind spots that affected its ability to identify and respond to increasing complaints about quality and unintended acceleration in a timely or sufficient manner.

Toyota, like most organizations, did not understand its operations as fully as it thought it did. The same often holds true for many organizations, HROs included. To better understand what is happening, it takes a continually updated package of core beliefs built into meaningful local practices that make denial and neglect difficult. Values matter, as do frames of reference, communication, and candor. Cultures that sustain performance in the face of complexity are significant accomplishments. That accomplishing takes more than the input of bright engineers and designers.

Sustaining Sustained Performance

"Human error is not a distinct category of human performance. After the outcome is clear, any attribution of error is a social and psychological judgment process, not a narrow, purely technical or objective analysis."[1]
—Richard I. Cook and David D. Woods

"Reliability is not bankable, nor contingent on how many failure-free performances lie behind."[2]

—Paul R. Schulman

"In a world of unexpected events the capability to make sense out of an emerging pattern is just as crucial as a highly refined system of decision making."[3]
—Karl E. Weick, Kathleen M. Sutcliffe, and David Obstfeld

H ere's the scene. It's December 2, 1984, at 11:30 PM, shortly before at least 3,800 people will die from a leak of a toxic gas, methyl isocyanate (MIC), at the Union Carbide pesticide plant in Bhopal, India.[4] An operator asks whether others can smell MIC in the air. The others say that the smell must be Flytox bug spray since the factory is not running. At 11:40 a control room operator joins the group that is sipping tea and announces that the pressure needle has suddenly jumped from 2 psi to 30 psi. This news is dismissed as a malfunctioning dial. At midnight some operators begin to experience watering eyes. Two operators walk out to storage tank number 610 to compare the pressure reading at the tank with the unusually high pressure reading in the control room. Both gauges give the same extreme readings. "As they watch the gauge, the operators feel the throbbing that occurs when a liquid is boiling and turning into a gas. 'There's a lot of movement going on in there.'"[5] The two spot a leak 8 yards off the ground at a drain cock, where they also see "a bubble of brownish water surrounded by a small cloud."[6] They report all of this back to the shift supervisor. The shift supervisor runs out to the tank, sees the growing cloud, and says simply, "It's not true."[7] What was "not true" was that an uncontrollable exothermic explosion of MIC was occurring in a plant that had been shut down six weeks earlier and was used solely for inert storage. The supervisor is confronted by a rare instance where nothing makes sense, not even a way to make sense. His plight is captured by Erving Goffman: "We can tolerate the unexplained, but not the inexplicable."[8]

Sustained Awareness

What seems inexplicable to the Bhopal supervisor contains a pattern that is basic to managing the unexpected. The pattern involves alertness, awareness, perception, and conception. Recall that "perception without conception is blind; conception without perception is empty."[9] The unexpected can escalate either when significant cues go unnoticed because there are no concepts to select them (problem of blindness) or when the concepts that people deploy have no connection to particulars (problem of emptiness). Crises worsen because of senseless details or meaningless conjectures. Both flaws were operating at Bhopal. Details of rumbling ground and bubbles of brownish water are senseless in a plant that is shut down. And the concept of a plant that no longer produces pesticides is meaningless when dials in a control room are fluctuating. The concepts don't inform the perceptions, and the perceptions can't be explained by the prevailing concepts.

Relationships between perception and conception have been invoked repeatedly in the preceding chapters. Those discussions were built on the theme that mindful organizing is focused on clear and detailed comprehension of emerging threats and on factors that interfere with such comprehension. Small failures have to be noticed (the principle of preoccupation with failure), and their distinctiveness must be retained rather than lost in a category (reluctance to simplify). People need to remain aware of ongoing operations if they want to notice nuances that could be symptoms of failure (sensitivity to operations). Attention is also crucial for locating pathways to recovery (commitment to resilience) and for knowing how to implement those pathways (deference to expertise). Faced with such demands, mindful organizations devote more time than other organizations to examining failure as a window on the health of the system, resisting the urge to simplify assumptions about the world, observing operations and their effects, developing resilience to manage unexpected events, and identifying local experts and creating a climate of deference to them.

Sustained Surfacing

Think back to a word we use quite often, the word *surface*. Mindful organizing treats that word as both a noun and a verb. As a *noun*, a surface means the things, texts, and topics that people talk about (e.g., a strange odor, a run on the bank, an ominous weather forecast). A surface is a tool that helps us understand what is going on (e.g., we have to cancel the Rail Fair) or to reflect concerns, wariness, and apprehensions (e.g., that accident in California worries me). Surface used as a *verb* means to make visible, make salient, give voice to, anomalize, and expose to view. To surface is to call attention to something and make it more difficult to dismiss or normalize it.

Both surfaces and surfacing are influenced by the shareability constraint, the concern that details get lost when they are converted into common descriptions. Robert Irwin argues that we surrender some of our "unique" experience so that we can "share, impart, partake, make known in common."[10] Irwin calls this loss of information an "active condensation." And the nature of that "loss" is an important determinant of reliable functioning. When you organize for higher reliability, you can't avoid condensation and substitution. But you can be more deliberate when you enrich the discourse that affects what stands out.

No matter how mindful you are of surfaces and surfacing, you'll still have a problem with accuracy. Here's the problem. When two people talk to one another, their worlds are different. But, "There can be no third version of the world that is more correct than these two; there can only be a third version of the world that explains to them why their versions differ. We are all experts in our own world."[11] That's why respectful interaction and heedful interrelating are so crucial for managing the unexpected. They enable equivalent understanding, which is an improvement on the belief that we have essentially common, shared understanding of non-obvious disruptions.

Sustained Organizing

Organizing creates organization out of generalizations, hindsight, and the conversion of knowledge by acquaintance into shared knowledge by description. We generalize in the interest of cohesion, but that generalizing can be costly if it encourages us to normalize anomalies. None of us can escape selective perception. Nor would we want to. But that selective perception can be redirected so that people try to capture nuance, refine distinctions, pay closer attention to particulars, and invent new categories. In short, we can enact selective perception more mindfully. Mindful action is accomplished by refining one's stock of concepts, by enlarging one's action repertoire, by more focus on relationships of respectful interaction and heedful interrelating, and by the implementation of principles for high reliability organizing.

That sounds more straightforward in theory than it is in practice. Organizing around reliability is complicated by paradoxes,[12] by practices that "contain contradictions yet may still be true and in accordance with the facts and common sense."[13] The property of paradox has been with us almost from the start of this book in the form of the idea of an "anomaly." The words *anomaly* and *paradox* are comparable because both of them "express an inherent contradiction."[14] Specifically, "an anomaly is something that is contrary to what it should be . . . [It may be] irreconcilable with its surroundings or conditions."[15]

Gene Rochlin neatly summarizes some of the paradoxes inherent in organizing for higher reliability. High reliability organizations (HROs) "seek an ideal of perfection but never expect to achieve it. They demand complete safety but never expect it. They dread surprise but always anticipate it. They deliver reliability but never take it for granted. They live by the book but are unwilling to die by it. . . . Such representational ambiguity is implicitly (and sometimes explicitly) acknowledged and accepted by the organization, not just as part of the cost of maintaining performance levels, but as an active contributor to problem solving."[16] A similar emphasis is evident in Todd LaPorte's counsel that if we want to create sustained performance, then "we must act when we cannot foresee consequences; we must plan when we cannot know; we must organize when we cannot control."[17] Our interpretation of these paradoxes is that HROs, unlike most organizations, are able simultaneously both to believe and to doubt their past experience.[18]

In a hospital emergency department, for example, one is never quite sure what will come through the doors next. All one can be sure of is that it will be some combination of ambiguity and clarity that will be met with some mixture of doubt and certainty that is turned into some combination of action, updating, and diagnosing. Routines and protocols impose some short-term certainties that momentarily silence some doubts, but other doubts remain.[19] The fate of those remaining doubts depends on the extent to which variety in the possibilities considered by the medical treatment team is sufficient to sense and comprehend the variety that they face.

Sustained Updating

If, as LaPorte says, paradoxes develop when we are unsure of consequences, knowledge, and control, then one way to manage is to practice mindful updating. This form of updating, which helps us act, plan, and organize, would follow a protocol like this:

1. Scrutinize small failures,
2. Refine the categories you impose,
3. Watch what you're doing and what emerges,

4. Make do with the resources you have, and

5. Listen.

What these processes can produce is ongoing adaptation as we keep asking, "What's the story?" Even though we keep asking this question, we do so knowing that there is no such thing as *the* story, nor is our current story static. As the present evolves, we need to keep asking, "*Now* what's the story?" Events change. We change. But, do our stories change? If they don't, then we lose variety and the capability to adapt. Marianne Paget summarizes the tension this way: "The work process unfolds as a series of approximations and attempts to discover an appropriate response. And because it unfolds this way, as an error-ridden activity, it requires continuous attention."[20]

We have often said that updating means "reconstituting an evolving present." The activities of organizing remain in motion, and these motions stir up details and meanings that might have been missed. Meanings help you make sense and regain or retain some control. The implicit advice is not to stop the action too quickly. People think by acting, and people think *while* acting, which is why their efforts to develop a sense of what is happening are described as sense*making*. It is these efforts that can escalate or defuse an unexpected event.

A convenient shorthand to crystallize the stopping and starting of action and the short-term consequences was suggested by the German philosopher Martin Heidegger.[21] When people act in the world, their circumstance is one of "absorbed coping," or *ready-to-hand engagement*. When people act in this engaged mode, they are aware of the world as a network of interrelated projects rather than as an arrangement of discrete physical objects and events. If one of those projects is interrupted, then their experience changes into an *unready-to-hand* mode. Problematic aspects of the situation stand out, but knowledge of the context and its interdependencies remains in place. The aspects that stand out are *not* stripped of context. It is only when people detach from the project and look backward in a *present-at-hand* mode that general, abstract, context-free analyses uncover what seem to be independent entities. Failures to manage the unexpected lurk not so much in the unready-to-hand interruption as they do in the loss of context, when people disassemble an event into its seeming parts and strip away meaningful interdependencies.

Sustained Agency

Interdependent people search for meaning, settle for plausibility, and move on. To manage the unexpected is to turn that sequence inside out and rework it with the goal of making anomalies more conspicuous and normalization more difficult. To manage the unexpected is to help people make sense and "to avoid the real disaster, which would be the incapacity to represent the event."[22]

Rear Admiral Tom Mercer, when he was the captain of the carrier *Carl Vinson* (CVN 70), was responsible to see that his ship did not lose its capacity to represent events. When members of the Berkeley research team (Gene Rochlin, Karlene Roberts, and Todd LaPorte) observed Mercer's carrier operations and described the carrier as a "high reliability organization."[23] Mercer said in effect, "That is what we're trying to do although I never put it that way." Notice what can happen when tacit, unverbalized efforts to act more reliably become more explicit. Now you can do things such as distribute those practices more widely, strengthen and prioritize them, include them more clearly in training and socialization, and weave them into conversations. That's a lot to claim for a phrase, HRO. But not when you incorporate it into practice.

And not when behavioral and social tendencies are being shaped. Consider the following. The context within which people take actions can compel them to search for diagnoses and explanations that serve to justify their actions. The problem is this mechanism can operate regardless of its effects on recovering from the unexpected. People often feel responsible for their actions when those actions are interpreted as chosen, irrevocable, and public.[24] This can lead to a biased search for explanations that justify those actions. These justifications may sound shallow, but they are useful to the agent and are acceptable in the eyes of some peers who matter to the agent.

There is an interesting twist to this mechanism. When *other* people observe what you do, those people can also make attributions about the choice, irrevocability, and publicness of what you did. This means that they can link you with actions that in fact look quite different to you. And they can press you to explain yourself and to adopt simple justifications that dumb down the complexity. As Weick and Sutcliffe show,[25] when the Bristol Royal Infirmary had a series of public, irrevocable pediatric deaths during heart surgery, using procedures for which there were safer alternatives, its prevailing explanation was that it was dealing with unusually complex cases. This justification, which was not substantiated by a review board, meant that there was less incentive for surgeons to learn and improve their technique or to review existing protocols and more incentive to believe and enact this misleading justification.[26]

To include these examples under the heading "Sustained Agency" is to make a larger point. Much of our analysis is focused at the micro and meso level of analysis. That is intentional because we want to make it clear that agency matters and that it can be enhanced in mindful organizing. For example, when people become more preoccupied with their justifications and the blind spots they create, then they create a capability that was not there before. They develop the capability for foresight and see more possibilities and more details. William James captures the nature of agency when he says, "I, for my part, cannot escape the consideration, forced upon me at every turn, that the knower is not simply a mirror floating with no foot-hold anywhere, and passively reflecting an order that he comes upon and finds simply existing. The knower is an actor, and coefficient of the truth on one side, whilst on the other he registers the truth which he helps to create. Mental interests, hypotheses, postulates, so far as they are bases for human action—action which to a great extent transforms the world—help to *make* the truth which they declare."[27] There is no place for a mere mirror when the goal is to manage the unexpected.

An example of a person and a style of leading that embodies a reflecting mirror and an enacting creator is the late Paul Gleason.[28] Gleason, at the time of the following description, was the crew superintendent of the 19-person Zig Zag Hotshot wildland firefighting crew. Gleason said that when fighting fires, he prefers to view his leadership efforts as sensemaking rather than decision making. In his words, "If I make a decision it is a possession, I take pride in it, I tend to defend it and not listen to those who question it. If I make sense, then this is more dynamic and I listen and I can change it. A decision is something you polish. Sensemaking is a direction for the next period." When Gleason perceives his work as decision making, he feels that he postpones action so he can get the decision right. And after he makes the decision, he finds himself defending it rather than revising it to suit changing circumstances. Polishing and defending eat up valuable time, preclude learning, and encourage blind spots. If, instead, Gleason treats an unfolding fire as a problem in sensemaking, then he gives his crew a direction, a direction which by definition is dynamic, open to revision at any time, self-correcting, responsive, and with more of its rationale being transparent. Polishing and defending a decision mobilizes justifications that necessarily favor some perceptions over others. Those blind spots were the very things that worried Gleason.

Sustained Variety

A microlevel perspective can foster the impression that we are all different. That is true but only up to a point. We notice different things, *but* we all notice. The things we notice are determined by our selective interests, *but* we all have interests. Whatever we notice shapes our experiences and what we claim is "the real world," *but* we all claim to know some kind of world. We have a wide range of feelings, *but* we all feel. We think different things, *but* "always by the same methods, those methods being that we observe, discriminate, generalize, classify, look for causes, trace analogies, and make hypotheses."[29] So the specific things we notice, the interests we pursue, the experiences we store away in stories, the feelings that animate us, and the thoughts we think are all different. *But* we are all similar in the sense that we all notice, select, narrate, feel, and think about our experiences.

Human nature is the source of interruptions to sustained performance, but it is also the source of higher sustained reliability. For example, we tend to ignore small deviations and treat them as close enough to normal so that we can move on. We forget that the deviations could be an indication of a larger problem or could interact with other small deviations and create a much larger problem (HRO principle 1). We tend to simplify what we see and underestimate how much crucial information we are losing (HRO principle 2). We tend to pay less attention to what is going on here and now in connected operations and what the consequences are for those who depend on us (HRO principle 3). We tend to presume that we already know enough to handle anything that comes along and forget that there are problems we have never seen or imagined (HRO principle 4). And finally, we defer to authority even when those in higher positions micromanage with low situation awareness and rusty skills (HRO principle 5).

To reverse these limiting tendencies, you can start with five guidelines that represent one attempt to summarize what other HROs have done.[30] Ask yourself, Can I alter our ways of working so that it is easier for people to puzzle over small disruptions, question familiar labels, understand what they're currently doing, enhance their options, and identify the expertise that is needed?

Sustained Change

At this point you may be thinking, "Now what? How do I change our culture to become more mindful?" That's the wrong question. The better question is, What problems am I trying to solve? In the words of Edgar Schein, never start with the idea of changing culture.[31] Always start with the issue the organization faces; only when those business issues are clear should you ask yourself whether the culture aids or hinders resolving the issues. What Schein has in mind is this: When thinking about change, think initially of the culture as your source of strength since past successes have affected it. Even if some elements of the culture look dysfunctional, remember that these are probably a small portion of a larger set of elements that continue to be strengths. If changes need to be made in how the organization is run, try to build on existing cultural strengths rather than attempting to change those elements that may be weaknesses.

There is lots of breathless talk these days about change, but behind it is a surprising reliance on basics that need to be reaffirmed. People have mistakenly concluded that since the pace of change has accelerated, the basics of change management must also change. The new hyperbole is about "disruption,"[32] and the new imperative is "change or die."[33]

We don't see it that way. Our emphasis on continuing adaptation and updating reduces the need for sudden, radical change. HROs seldom have to play catch up. Remember, they have to maintain their own variety to manage the variety they face and sustain performance. Continuing adaptation occurs as long as there is a workable, shared set of beliefs that (1) animates people and gets them moving and experimenting; (2) provides a direction; (3) encourages updating through closer attention to what is happening; and (4) facilitates respectful interaction, which enables people to build a more stable picture of what they face. The question for any program of planned change is the extent to which it engages or blocks these four. Our position is that there is nothing special about the content of specific change programs that explains their success or failure. Instead, what matters is the extent to which the program triggers sustained animation, direction, attention, and respectful interaction. It is these four practices that make it easier or harder for people to make sense collectively of what they currently face and to deal with it.

Consider what happens to these four in a conventional change intervention. When a new program is imposed on people, they have to keep the business going the old way while they get accustomed to running it the new way. When they try to do this, their work often becomes more ambiguous. Working the old way is simultaneously good (it maintains continuity) and bad (it resists new practices). Resolving the ambiguity is tough because people find it harder to act to test hunches, harder to identify a general direction that allows local adaptation, and harder to converse candidly in ways that build a consensual picture of what is happening. If the ambiguity persists, this becomes increasingly stressful, which has the unfortunate effect of forcing people to fall back onto overlearned earlier routines that are the very tendencies the change initiative was supposed to abolish.

In the preceding chapters we have suggested that an early step in a change effort is to use gentle audits to help you get a feel for where you stand with regard to each principle. We use the adjective *gentle* because we are more worried about the severe audits that Patrick Lagadec calls "brutal audits." Brutal audits are the ones that should haunt you and guide your efforts to prepare for surprises. "The ability to deal with a crisis situation is largely dependent on the structures that have been developed before chaos arrives. The event can in some ways be considered as an abrupt and brutal audit: at a moment's notice, everything that was left unprepared becomes a complex problem, and every weakness comes rushing to the forefront. The breech in the defences opened by crisis creates a sort of vacuum."[34]

Conclusion

Our goal has been to enable organizing that produces dynamic nonevents. A dynamic event is a potentially disabling surprise. A nonevent is a million accidents waiting to happen that don't. We are interested in performance reliability in context and in getting people to think differently, a little earlier, to decrease the vulnerability of systems and increase system capability and learning.

Think about what you do most of the time. You converse and text and present and anticipate. It is not a big leap to say that "organization is realized in moments of conversation and joint action that are embedded in day-to-day interactions."[35] As James Taylor and Elizabeth Van Every explained in Chapter 2, your actions basically turn circumstances into a situation that is comprehensible and that serves as a springboard for action. That description is filled with action. There are the actions of turning flux into circumstances, turning circumstances into a comprehensible situation, turning comprehension into a direction and an intention, and turning those intentions into their realization. It is tempting to go through that sequence mindlessly. But there are alternatives. Some of them are in front of you.

Notes

Preface

1. Todd R. LaPorte, "On Vectors and Retrospection: Reflections on Understanding Public Organizations," *Journal of Contingencies and Crisis Management* 19, no. 1 (2011): 62.

Chapter 1

1. Terry Winograd and Fernando Flores, *Understanding Computers and Cognition: A New Foundation for Design* (Boston: Addison-Wesley Professional, 1987), 165.
2. Friedrich Nietzsche, *Twilight of the Idols* (Baltimore: Penguin Books, 1968), 3, italics in original.
3. The phrase *high reliability organization* was coined by Berkeley researchers Karlene Roberts, Gene Rochlin, and Todd LaPorte to capture observed commonalities of operations among the carrier *Carl Vinson* (CVN-70); the Federal Aviation Administration en route Air Traffic Control in Fremont, California; and the Diablo Canyon nuclear power generation plant at San Luis Obispo, California. See Gene Rochlin, Todd LaPorte, and Karlene Roberts, "The Self-Designing High Reliability Organization: Aircraft Carrier Flight Operation at Sea," *Naval War College Review* 40 (1987): 76–90 and Karlene Roberts, "Some Characteristics of High Reliability Organizations," *Organization Science* 1 (1990): 160–177. In settings such as these, HROs operate in an unforgiving environment rich with the potential for error, where the scale of consequences precludes learning through experimentation and where complex processes are used to manage complex technology to avoid failures. See Karl E. Weick and Kathleen M. Sutcliffe, *Managing the Unexpected: Resilient Performance in an Age of*

Uncertainty, 2nd ed. (San Francisco: Jossey-Bass, 2007), footnote 30, 164–166.

4. Emery Roe and Paul R. Schulman, *High Reliability Management: Operating on the Edge* (Stanford, CA: Stanford University Press, 2008), 228–233.

5. Michael D. Cohen, "Reading Dewey: Reflections on the Study of Routine," *Organization Studies* 28, no. 5 (2007): 773–786.

6. For an additional analysis of the financial industry from an HRO perspective, see Karlene H. Roberts and Carolyn Libuser, "From Bhopal to Banking: Organizational Design Can Mitigate Risk," *Organizational Dynamics* 21, no. 4 (1993): 15–26.

7. Langdon Winner, "Complexity and the Limits of Human Understanding," in *Organized Social Complexity*, ed. Todd R. LaPorte (Princeton, NJ: Princeton University, 1975), 40–76, see 69.

8. Todd R. LaPorte, "Complexity and Uncertainty: Challenge to Action," in *Organized Social Complexity*, ed. Todd R. LaPorte (Princeton, NJ: Princeton University, 1975), 332–356, see 353.

9. The concept of weak signals is discussed more fully in Diane Vaughan, "Signals and Interpretive Work: The Role of Culture in a Theory of Practical Action," in *Culture in Mind: Toward a Sociology of Culture and Cognition*, ed. Karen A. Cerulo. (New York: Routledge, 2002), 28–54.

10. Kirsten Grind, *The Lost Bank: The Story of Washington Mutual—The Biggest Bank Failure in American History* (New York: Simon and Schuster, 2012). This analysis also draws on Carl Levin and Tom Coburn, *Wall Street and the Financial Crisis: Anatomy of a Financial Collapse* (Washington, DC: Permanent Subcommittee on Investigations, April 13, 2011).

11. Grind, *The Lost Bank*, 23. Also see Karl E. Weick, "What is the Academy Reading? One Answer," *Academy of Management Review*, 38, no. 2 (2013): 318–323, for an analysis of this book that is framed in terms of organizational theory.

12. Grind, *The Lost Bank*, 52.

13. Ibid., 67.

14. Ibid., 187.

15. Ibid., 148.

16. Ibid., 146.

17. Ibid., 57.

18. Ibid., 125.

19. Levin and Coburn, *Wall Street*, 91–92.

20. Ibid., 123.

21. Ibid., 135.

22. Ibid., 176.

23. It is interesting that this letter addresses all five HRO principles: It says the current system isn't working (failure), this is not growth but rather a bubble (simplification), you need a COO (operations), you are losing good people (resilience), and you're not competent as a COO (expertise).

24. Eventually a real New York banker (Steve Rotella) was brought in as COO; see Grind, *The Lost Bank*, 107.

25. Ibid., 239.

26. Ibid., 165.

27. Ibid., 150.

28. Ibid., 151.

29. Ibid., 161.

30. Ibid., 69.

31. Ibid., 166.

32. Barry A. Turner had first discussed this emergent patterning in 1978. See Barry A. Turner, *Man-Made Disasters* (London: Wykeham Publications, 1978).

33. In the remainder of the book, we often use the acronym FSORE as shorthand for the five principles that focus on failures, simplification, operations, resilience, and expertise.

34. Grind, *The Lost Bank*, 145.

35. Donald Palmer, *Normal Organizational Wrongdoing: A Critical Analysis of Theories of Misconduct in and by Organizations* (Oxford, United Kingdom: Oxford University Press, 2012), 229–235. See also Donald Palmer and Michael W. Maher, "The Mortgage Meltdown as Normal Accident Wrongdoing," *Strategic Organization* 8, no. 1 (2010): 83–89.

36. Grind, *The Lost Bank*, 172.

37. Ibid., 134.

38. Ibid., 157.

39. Ibid., 181.

40. Ibid., 177.

41. Ibid., 152, 170, 185, and 206.

42. Ibid., 66.

43. Ibid., 163.

44. Ibid., 60.

45. Ibid., 163.

46. Levin and Coburn, *Wall Street*, 66.

47. Grind, *The Lost Bank*, 171.

48. See Levin and Coburn, *Wall Street*, 104–107, for details of Jenne's report.

49. Levin and Coburn, *Wall Street*, 104.

50. Ibid., 108.

51. Grind, *The Lost Bank*, 156.

52. Ibid., 91.

53. Levin and Coburn, *Wall Street*, 87.

54. Grind, *The Lost Bank*, 165.

55. Ibid., 99.

56. Ibid., 100.

57. Ibid., 165.

58. Levin and Coburn, *Wall Street*, 87.

59. Grind, *The Lost Bank*, 200.

60. Ibid., 200.

61. OTS refers to the Office of Thrift Supervision.

62. OTS, "Compliance Management Program," (May 31, 2007), quoted in Levin and Coburn, *Wall Street*, 88.

63. Levin and Coburn, *Wall Street*, 114.

64. Grind, *The Lost Bank*, 151.

65. Erik Hollnagel, "Resilience: The Challenge of the Unstable," in *Resilience Engineering: Concepts and Precepts*, ed. Erik Hollnagel, David Woods, and Nancy Leveson (Burlington, VT: Ashgate, 2006), 9–18, see 16.

66. Grind, *The Lost Bank*, 99.

67. Levin and Coburn, *Wall Street*, 81.

68. Grind, *The Lost Bank*, 154.

69. Ibid., 173.

70. Ibid., 175.

71. Karlene H. Roberts, Susanne K. Stout, and Jennifer J. Halpern, "Decision Dynamics in Two High Reliability Military Organizations," *Management Science* 40 (1994): 614–624, see 622.

72. Grind, *The Lost Bank*, 150; see also Levin and Coburn, *Wall Street*, 110–111.

73. Grind, *The Lost Bank*, 149.

74. Ibid., 150; see also Levin and Coburn, *Wall Street*, 110–111.

75. Grind, *The Lost Bank*, 163.

76. Ibid., 151.

77. Levin and Coburn, *Wall Street*, 115.

78. Ibid., 102.

79. We often use the word *flux* to describe this condition.

80. Brian J. Kylén, "What Business Leaders Do—Before They Are Surprised," *Advances in Strategic Management* 3 (1985): 181–222.

81. Turner, *Man-Made Disasters*, 166.

Chapter 2

1. Yiannis Gabriel, *Organizing Words: A Critical Thesaurus for Social and Organization Studies* (New York: Oxford University Press, 2008), 212.

2. William James, "Pragmatism," *William James: Writings 1902–1910* (New York: Library of America, 1987), 513.

3. Identification of some of these "larger problems" is found in Nancy G. Leveson, "Applying Systems Thinking to Analyze and Learn from Events," *Safety Science* 49, no. 1 (2011): 55–64.

4. Charles Perrow, *Normal Accidents: Living with High-Risk Technologies* (New York: Basic Books, 1984).

5. Karl E. Weick, Kathleen M. Sutcliffe, and David Obstfeld, "Organizing for High Reliability: Processes of Collective Mindfulness," in *Research in Organizational Behavior*, ed. Barry M. Staw and Robert I. Sutton (Greenwich, CT: JAI Press, 1999), 21: 81–123.

6. This example is adapted from research of and selections in Marlys K. Christianson, Maria T. Farkas, Kathleen M. Sutcliffe, and Karl E. Weick, "Learning Through Rare Events: Significant Interruptions at the Baltimore & Ohio Railroad Museum," *Organization Science* 20, no. 5 (2009): 846–860.

7. The Presidents' Day weekend (February 15–18) snowstorm in 2003 set a new snowfall record for Baltimore, MD, with a total of 28.2 inches of snow (National Centers for Environmental Information, "Historic Storms," accessed June 1, 2015, http://www.ncdc.noaa.gov/snow-and-ice/rsi/historic-storms).

8. Michelle A. Barton and Kathleen M. Sutcliffe, "Overcoming Dysfunctional Momentum: Organizational Safety as a Social Achievement," *Human Relations* 62, no. 9 (2009): 1327–1356, see 1329.

9. William R. Rockey and Pamela S. Coleman, "The Rebirth of Baldwin's Cathedral," *Civil Engineering* 75, no. 2 (2005): 52–63.

10. B&O Railroad Museum, "History of the Museum," Accessed September 15, 2007, http://www.borail.org/History-of-the-Museum.aspx.

11. Ibid.

12. B&O Railroad Museum, *Annual Report 2002*, Accessed September 15, 2007, http://www.borail.org/pdf/2002_annual_report.pdf (site discontinued); B&O Railroad Museum, *Annual Report 2003*, Accessed on September 15, 2007, http://www.borail.org/pdf/2003_annual_report.pdf (site discontinued).

13. B&O Railroad Museum, "Baltimore & Ohio (B&O) Railroad Museum cancels the Fair of the Iron Horse 175, Festival of Trains," news release, February 28, 2003, http://www.prnewswire.co.uk/news-releases/baltimore—

ohio-bo-railroad-museum-cancels-the-fair-of-the-iron-horse-175-festival-of-trains-154544135.html.

14. Courtney Wilson, interview, October 16, 2006. http://www.wbaltv.com/news/maryland/baltimore-city/B-O-Railroad-Museum-thriving-10-years-after-roof-collapse/18565686.

15. Karl E. Weick, *Sensemaking in Organizations* (Thousand Oaks, CA: Sage, 1995), 145–154.

16. Our discussion of properties of expectations draws on James M. Olson, Neal J. Roese, and Mark P. Zanna, "Expectancies," in *Social Psychology: Handbook of Basic Principles*, ed. E. Tory Higgins and Arie W. Kruglanski (New York: Guilford Press, 1996).

17. In this chapter we treat expectations and expectancies as synonyms, and use the word *expectation* unless material that is quoted uses the word *expectancy*, as is true in this case.

18. John Dewey, *Human Nature and Conduct* (New York: Henry Holt, 1922), 178–179.

19. Wilson interview.

20. Barbara Czarniawska, "Karl Weick: Concepts, Style, and Reflection," supplement, *Sociological Review* 53, no. S1 (2005): 267–278, see 271.

21. James, "Pragmatism," 783.

22. Ibid., 1008–1009, italics in original.

23. James Miller, *Examined Lives: From Socrates to Nietzsche* (New York: Farrar, Strauss and Giroux, 2011), 268–273. Kant wrote, "What we can know about anything we perceive is determined [as much] by the categories and concepts we construct to use in our inquiries, as by our sentient experience of the world" (p. 273). Both parts are essential for the formula that guides the first critique: "Thoughts without content are empty, intuitions without concepts are blind."

24. James R. Taylor and Elizabeth J. Van Every, *The Emergent Organization: Communication as Its Site and Surface* (Mahwah, NJ: Erlbaum, 2000), 40.

25. Reuben M. Baron and Stephen J. Misovich, "On the Relationship Between Social and Cognitive Modes of Organization," in *Dual-Process Theories in Social Psychology*, ed. Shelly Chaiken and Yaacov Trope (New York: Guilford Press, 1999), 587.

26. We do not mean that knowledge by acquaintance is solitary and knowledge by description is social. All knowledge is an outcome of socialization and social interaction. What we mean by "takes a different form" is that concepts, labels, and descriptions that are firm-specific force people to ignore much of the firsthand flux that would be preserved by other less firm-specific substitutions. For example, curators of rare railroad artifacts bristle and become tense when moneymaking, catered events are held

among their exhibits. The exhibits bear the wear and tear of people partying, not people interested in history.

27. Ellen J. Langer, "Minding Matters: The Consequences of Mindlessness-Mindfulness," in *Advances in Experimental Social Psychology*, ed. Leonard Berkowitz (San Diego: Academic Press, 1989), 22: 138, 157, 159.

28. Gerald R. Salancik and Jeffrey Pfeffer, "Who Gets Power—And How They Hold on to It: A Strategic-Contingency Model of Power," *Organizational Dynamics* 5, no. 3 (1978): 3–21, 18–19, italics added.

29. Gabriel, *Organizing Words*, 212.

30. Haridimos Tsoukas, *Complex Knowledge: Studies in Organizational Epistemology* (Oxford, United Kingdom: Oxford, 2005), 124, italics added.

31. Taylor and Van Every, *The Emergent Organization*, 243.

32. Gabriel, *Organizing Words*, 211.

33. The cumulative and disruptive effects of the loss of this trust are vividly described in Kimberly Elsbach, Ileana Stigliani, and Amy Stroud, "The Building of Employee Distrust: A Case Study of Hewlett-Packard from 1995 to 2010," *Organizational Dynamics* 41, no. 3 (2012): 254–263.

34. Donald T. Campbell, "Asch's Moral Epistemology for Socially Shared Knowledge," in *The Legacy of Solomon Asch: Essays in Cognition and Social Psychology*, ed. Irvin Rock. (Hillsdale, NJ: Erlbaum, 1990), 39–52.

35. Ruth Blatt, Marlys K. Christianson, Kathleen M. Sutcliffe, and Marilynn M Rosenthal, "A Sensemaking Lens on Reliability," *Journal of Organizational Behavior* 27, no. 7 (2006): 897–917.

36. Robert Chia, "The Aim of Management Education: Reflections on Mintzberg's 'Managers not MBAs,'" *Organization Studies* 26, no. 7 (2005): 1092.

37. Gary Klein, *Intuition at Work: Why Developing Your Gut Instincts Will Make You Better at What You Do* (New York: Doubleday, 2003): 201–207.

38. Wilson interview.

39. Ibid.

40. Ibid.

41. This pattern of similar responses made to differing demands is a marker of organizational learning. Karl E. Weick, "The Nontraditional Quality of Organizational Learning," *Organization Science* 2, no. 1 (1991): 116–124.

42. Christianson et al., "Learning Through Rare Events."

43. Timothy J. Vogus, "In Search of Mechanisms: How Do HR Practices Affect Organizational Performance?," (PhD diss., University of Michigan, 2004): 138–148. A validation analysis of the MOS can be found in Timothy J. Vogus and Kathleen M. Sutcliffe, "The Safety Organizing Scale: Development and Validation of a Behavioral Measure of Safety Culture in Hospital Nursing Units," *Medical Care* 45, no. 1 (2007): 46–54.

Validation refers to the extent to which a measure purportedly measures what it is supposed to measure. Vogus and Sutcliffe found that the nine-item measure of self-reported behaviors had high internal reliability and discriminated between related concepts such as organizational commitment and trust. Moreover, high scores on the MOS were associated with lower levels of reported medication errors and patient falls in the period after the original survey was conducted. In a related paper titled "The Impact of Safety Organizing, Supportive Leadership, and Care Pathways on Reported Medication Errors in Hospital Nursing Units," *Medical Care* 45, no. 10 (2007): 997–1002, Vogus and Sutcliffe reported that a one-point increase in mindful organizing on a seven-point scale resulted in almost a 30 percent decrease in the expected number of medication errors six months later. Also see Dietmar Ausserhofer, M. Schubert, M. Blegen, S. De Geest, and R. Schwendimann, "Validity and Reliability on Three European Language Versions of the Safety Organizing Scale," *International Journal for Quality in Health Care* 25, no. 2 (2013): 157–166.

Chapter 3

1. Edgar Morin, *Seven Complex Lessons in Education for the Future* (Paris: UNESCO, 1999), 45.

2. For a discussion of failure, developed from the perspective of resilience engineering, see David D. Woods and Matthieu Branlat, "Basic Patterns in How Adaptive Systems Fail," in *Resilience Engineering in Practice: A Guidebook*, ed. Erik Hollnagel, Jean Paries, David W. Woods, and John Wreathall. (Burlington, VT: Ashgate, 2012), 127–144.

3. *The American Heritage Dictionary of the English Language*, 3rd ed., s.v. "anomaly." (New York: Houghton Mifflin, 1992), 75.

4. William James, *Principles of Psychology*, (Cambridge, MA: Harvard University Press, 1981), 1: 233.

5. Presidential Commission on the Space Shuttle Challenger Accident, *Report of the Presidential Commission on the Space Shuttle Challenger Accident* (Washington, DC: U.S. Government Printing Office, 1986), 1: 148. The complete quotation reads, "4. NASA's system for tracking anomalies for Flight Readiness Reviews failed in that, despite a history of persistent O-ring erosion and blow-by, flight was still permitted. It failed again in the strange sequence of six consecutive launch constraint waivers prior to 51-L, permitting it to fly without any record of a waiver, or even of an explicit constraint. Tracking and continuing only anomalies that are 'outside the data base' of prior flight allowed major problems to be removed from, and lost by, the reporting system."

6. Richard I. Cook and David D. Woods, "Operating at the Sharp End: The Complexity of Human Error," in *Human Error in Medicine*, Human Error and Safety, ed. Marilyn Sue Bogner. (Mahwah, NJ: Erlbaum, 1994), 274.

7. Vaughan, "Signals and Interpretive Work", 28–54.

8. Marianne A. Paget, *The Unity of Mistakes: A Phenomenological Interpretation of Medical Work* (Philadelphia, PA: Temple University Press, 1988), 56.

9. David D. Woods, Sidney Dekker, Richard Cook, Leila Johannsson, and Nadine Sarter, *Behind Human Error*, 2nd ed. (Burlington, VT: Ashgate, 2010), 117–121.

10. Diane Vaughan, *The Challenger Launch Decision: Risky Technology, Culture, and Deviance at NASA* (Chicago: University of Chicago Press, 1996), 392–393.

11. Vaughan, *The Challenger Launch Decision*, 124, 141, 143, 179.

12. Quoted in ibid., 249.

13. Paul R. Schulman, "General Attributes of Safe Organizations," supplement, *Quality and Safety in Health Care* 13, no. S2 (2004): 39–44.

14. James Reason, "Human Error: Models and Management," *British Medical Journal* 320 (2000): 768–770; The following description of the Swiss Cheese Model is found in Department of Community and Family Medicine, Duke University Medical Center, "Swiss Cheese Model" accessed February 15, 2007, http://patientsafetyed.duhs.duke.edu/module_e/swiss_cheese.html: In the swiss cheese model of system failure:

Every step in a process has the potential for failure, to varying degrees. The ideal system is analogous to a stack of slices of Swiss cheese. Consider the holes to be opportunities for a process to fail, and each of the slices as "defensive layers" in the process. An error may allow a problem to pass through a hole in one layer, but in the next layer the holes are in different places, and the problem should be caught. Each layer is a *defense* against potential error impacting the outcome. For a catastrophic error to occur, the holes need to align for each step in the process allowing all defenses to be defeated and resulting in an error. If the layers are set up with all the holes lined up, this is an inherently flawed system that will allow a problem at the beginning to progress all the way through to adversely affect the outcome. Each slice of cheese is an opportunity to stop an error. The more defenses you put up, the better. Also the fewer the holes and the smaller the holes, the more likely you are to catch/stop errors that may occur.

15. William H. Starbuck and Frances J. Milliken, "Challenger: Fine-Tuning the Odds Until Something Breaks," *Journal of Management Studies* 25, no. 4 (1988): 319–340. A number of other scholars have documented the liabilities of success. See for example Danny Miller, "The Architecture of

Simplicity," *Academy of Management Review* 18 (1993): 116–138 and Sim B. Sitkin, "Learning through Failure: The Strategy of Small Losses," in *Research in Organizational Behavior*, ed. Barry M. Staw and L. L. Cummings (Greenwich, CT: JAI Press, 1992), 14: 231–266.

16. Larry Heimann, "Repeated Failures in the Management of High Risk Technologies," *European Management Journal* 23, no. 1 (2005), 105–117, see 112.

17. Heimann, "Repeated Failures," 115.

18. John Dewey, *Human Nature and Conduct*.

19. U.S. Fire Administration, FEMA, *U.S. Fire Administration/Technical Report Series: Four Firefighters Die in Seattle Warehouse Fire* (Emmitsburg, MD: U.S. Fire Administration, USFA-TR-077/January 1995), 1, 14, 18, 23–24.

20. Eric-Hans Kramer, *Organizing Doubt: Grounded Theory, Army Units and Dealing with Dynamic Complexity* (Copenhagen, Denmark: Copenhagen Business School Press, 2007).

21. Kramer, *Organizing Doubt*, 17.

22. Ibid., 17–18.

23. Ibid., 135.

24. Karl E. Weick, *The Social Psychology of Organizing*, 1st ed., Topics in Social Psychology (Reading, MA: Addison-Wesley, 1969), 60. See also the second edition, 1979, 224–228.

25. Columbia Accident Investigation Board, *Columbia Accident Investigation Board: Report, Volume One* (Washington, DC: Government Printing Office, 2003), 190.

26. James T. Reason, *Managing the Risks of Organizational Accidents* (Brookfield, VT: Ashgate, 1997), 37.

27. Paul E. Bierly and J. C. Spender, "Culture and High Reliability Organizations: The Case of the Nuclear Submarine," *Journal of Management* 21, no. 4 (1995): 644.

28. For a recent summary of this work, see the 79 chapters in Kim S. Cameron and Gretchen M. Spreitzer, eds., *The Oxford Handbook of Positive Organizational Scholarship*, Oxford Library of Psychology (New York: Oxford University Press, 2011). See Chapter 50, 664–676, "Mindful Organizing" and Chapter 64, 843–854, "Managing the Unexpected." For a sampler of POS work focused on organizations, see the special issue of *Organizational Dynamics* 41, no. 2 (2012), ed. Gretchen Spreitzer and Kim Cameron.

29. Reason, *Managing the Risks of Organizational Accidents*, 25.

30. Karen A. Cerulo, *Never Saw It Coming: Cultural Challenges to Envisioning the Worst* (Chicago: University of Chicago Press, 2008), 6.

31. *Webster's New Dictionary of Synonyms*, s.v. "reliability" (Springfield, MA: Merriam-Webster, 1984).

32. "Foreign Object Damage," accessed February 10, 2014. http://www.sizor.com/cvn65/f18/fod_walk.html (site discontinued).

33. CNBC, "Boeing's Dreamliner Nightmare: PR Fail or Tech Mess?," November 15, 2013, http://www.cnbc.com/id/101178693.

34. BBC, "Boeing 787 Aircraft Grounded After Battery Problem in Japan," January 14, 2014, http://www.bbc.com/news/business-25737515.

35. Cerulo, *Never Saw It Coming*, 6.

36. Barton and Sutcliffe, "Overcoming Dysfunctional Momentum," 1329.

37. Ron Westrum, "Cultures with Requisite Imagination," in *Verification and Validation of Complex Systems: Human Factors Issues*, Nato ASI Subseries F, ed. John A. Wise, V. David Hopkin, and Paul Stager, vol. 110 (Berlin: Springer-Verlag, 1992), 402–405.

38. The example comes from Gary Klein, *Sources of Power: How People Make Decisions* (Cambridge, MA: The MIT Press, 1998), 66.

39. See Mark R. Chassin and Elise C. Becher, "The Wrong Patient," *Annals of Internal Medicine* 136, no. 11 (2002): 826–833.

40. For a more managerial discussion of recognizing and preventing near misses, see Catherine Tinsley, Robin L. Dillon, and Peter M. Madsen, "How to Avoid Catastrophe," *Harvard Business Review* 89, no. 4 (2011): 90–97.

Chapter 4

1. David Winter, "Bye, Bye, Theory, Goodbye," review of *Elegy for Theory*, by D. N. Rodowick, *Los Angeles Review of Books*, January 16, 2014, http://lareviewofbooks.org/review/bye-bye-theory-goodbye/.

2. National Commission on Terrorist Attacks upon the United States, *The 9/11 Commission Report: Final Report of the National Commission on Terrorist Attacks upon the United States* (Washington, DC: Government Printing Office, 2011), 343. Observation by the Counterterrorism Center before 9/11.

3. Elliot Massie, "Elliott Massie's Learning Trends: Learning, Training, Technology & Change," June 3, 2010, http://trends.masie.com/archives/2010/6/3/626-speech-therapy-by-video-admiral-thad-allen-and-leadershi.html. While serving as Coast Guard chief of staff, Thad Allen, the speaker of this quote, was placed in charge of search and rescue operations after Hurricane Katrina in September 2005 and was in charge of onsite relief efforts. The Coast Guard has often been cited for its extraordinary effectiveness as a first responder at Katrina. See for example John C. Morris, Elizabeth D. Morris, and Dale M. Jones, "Reaching for the

Philosopher's Stone: Contingent Coordination and the Military's Response to Hurricane Katrina," supplement, *Public Administration Review* 67, no. S1 (2007): 94–106.

4. Paraphrased from. Ian McCammon, "Heuristic Traps in Recreational Avalanche Accidents: Evidence and Implications," *Avalanche News* 68, no. 1 (2004): 42–50.

5. Paraphrased from. John Law, "Ladbroke Grove, Or How to Think about Failing Systems," Lancaster LA1 4YN, the Centre for Science Studies, Lancaster University, United Kingdom, December 6, 2003, http://www.lancaster.ac.uk/sociology/research/publications/papers/law-ladbroke-grove-failing-systems.pdf.

6. Paul R. Schulman, "The Negotiated Order of Organizational Reliability," *Administration & Society* 25, no. 3 (1993): 353–372, see 364.

7. Tor Hernes, *Understanding Organization as Process: Theory for a Tangled World* (New York: Routledge, 2007), 36.

8. Karl E. Weick, "Managing the Unexpected: Complexity as Distributed Sensemaking," in *Uncertainty and Surprise in Complex Systems: Questions on Working with the Unexpected*, ed. Reuben R. McDaniel and Dean J. Driebe (New York: Springer, 2005), 51–65.

9. Madeline Drexler, *Secret Agents: The Menace of Emerging Infections* (Washington, DC: Joseph Henry Press, 2002), 56.

10. Karl E. Weick, "Making Sense of Blurred Images: Mindful Organizing in Mission STS-107," in *Organization at the Limit: Lessons from the Columbia Disaster*, ed. William H. Starbuck and Moshe Farjoun (Malden, MA: Blackwell, 2005), 159–178.

11. Columbia Accident Investigation Board, *Columbia Accident Investigation Board*, 181.

12. Ron Westrum, "Thinking by Groups, Organizations, and Networks: A Sociologist's View of the Social Psychology of Science and Technology," in *The Social Psychology of Science*, Conduct of Science, ed. William R. Shadish and Steve Fuller. (New York: Guilford Press, 1993), 329–342, 340.

13. W. Ross Ashby, "Requisite Variety and Its Implications for the Control of Complex Systems," *Cybernetica* 1 (1958): 83–99. Chadwick J. Haberstroh (1965) describes requisite variety this way: "If the environment can disturb a system in a wide variety of ways, then effective control requires a regulator that can sense these disturbances and intervene with a commensurately large repertory of responses" (see 1176). Chadwick J. Haberstroh, "Organization Design and Systems Analysis," in *Handbook of Organizations*, ed. James G. March. (Chicago: Rand McNally, 1965), 1171–1212.

14. Mary Uhl-Bien, Russ Marion, and Bill McKelvey, "Complexity Leadership Theory: Shifting Leadership from the Industrial Age to the

Knowledge Era," *The Leadership Quarterly* 18, no. 4 (2007): 298–318. Also see Sean T. Hannah, Robert G. Lord, and Craig L. Pearce, "Leadership and Collective Requisite Complexity," *Organizational Psychology Review* 1, no. 3 (2011): 215–238.

15. Uhl-Bien, Marion, and McKelvey, "Complexity Leadership Theory," 302.

16. Hannah, Lord, and Pearce, "Leadership and Collective Requisite Complexity," 219.

17. Robert G. Lord, Sean T. Hannah, and Peter L. Jennings, "A Framework for Understanding Leadership and Individual Requisite Complexity," *Organizational Psychology Review* 1, no. 2 (2011): 108.

18. Jeroen Wolbers and Kees Boersma, "The Common Operational Picture as Collective Sensemaking," *Journal of Contingencies and Crisis Management* 21, no. 4 (2013): 186–199.

19. Gene I. Rochlin, "Informal Organizational Networking as a Crisis-Avoidance Strategy: US Naval Flight Operations as a Case Study," *Organization and Environment* 3 (1989): 159–176.

20. Kramer, *Organizing Doubt*, 74–75.

21. Weick, *The Social Psychology of Organizing*, 2nd ed., 17–18.

22. Cohen, "Reading Dewey," 781–782. See also Scott F. Turner and Violina Rindova, "A Balancing Act: How Organizations Pursue Consistency in Routine Functioning in the Face of Ongoing Change," *Organization Science* 23, no. 1 (2012): 24–46.

23. Roe and Schulman, *High Reliability Management*, 55.

24. Gilbert Ryle, *On Thinking*, ed. Konstantin Kolenda (New York: Rowman & Littlefield, 1980), 129.

25. Jenny W. Rudolph, J. Bradley Morrison, and John Carroll, "The Dynamics of Action-Oriented Problem Solving: Linking Interpretation and Choice," *Academy of Management Review* 34, no. 4 (2009): 733–756, see 740.

26. Rudolph, Morrison, and Carroll, "The Dynamics of Action-Oriented Problem Solving," 737.

27. Ibid., 748.

28. Lee Clarke, "The Disqualification Heuristic: When Do Organizations Misperceive Risk?," *Research in Social Problems and Public Policy* 5 (1993): 289–312. The basic idea is that people disqualify disconfirming information, highlight confirming information, and neglect information that contradicts a conviction, all in the interest of reducing uncertainty and increasing a sense of control.

29. Schulman, "General Attributes of Safe Organizations," 40.

30. John A. Meacham, "The Loss of Wisdom," in *Wisdom: Its Nature, Origins, and Development*, ed. Robert J. Sternberg. (New York: Cambridge University Press, 1990), 181–211, see 185, 187.

31. Meacham, "The Loss of Wisdom," 210.

32. This phrase is quoted in Lawrence Weschler and Robert Irwin, *Seeing is Forgetting the Name of the Thing One Sees: A Life of Contemporary Artist Robert Irwin* (Berkeley, CA: University of California Press, 1982).

33. V. De Keyser and David D. Woods, "Fixation Errors: Failures to Revise Situation Assessment in Dynamic and Risky Systems," in *Systems Reliability Assessment: Proceedings of the Ispra Course . . .* , Ispra Courses, ed. A. G. Colombo and Amalio Saiz de Bustamante, vol. 6 (Dordrechts, Netherlands: Kluwer Academic, 1990), 231–251.

34. Klein, *Sources of Power*, 274.

Chapter 5

1. Richard I. Cook and David D. Woods, "Operating at the Sharp End," 293.

2. Karl Weick's personal communication with confidential source April 5, 2012.

3. Andrew Hopkins, *Managing Major Hazards: The Lessons of the Moura Mine Disaster* (Sydney, Australia: Allen & Unwin, 2001), 9.

4. This example is from John Dill, "Staying Alive," accessed January 2015, http://www.friendsofyosar.org/safety/climbingSafety.html.

5. Columbia Accident Investigation Board, *Columbia Accident Investigation Board*, 202.

6. Paul R. Schulman, "The Analysis of High Reliability Organizations: A Comparative Framework," in *New Challenges to Understanding Organization*, ed. Karlene Roberts. (New York: Macmillan, 1993), 33–54, see 43.

7. There is a certain amount of irrevocability in operations as John Dewey makes clear in his concept of the "continuity of experience": "The basic characteristic of habit is that every experience enacted and undergone modifies the one who acts and undergoes . . . (T)his modification affects, whether we wish it or not, the quality of subsequent experience. For it is a somewhat different person who enters into them . . . (T)he principle of continuity of experience means that every experience both takes up something from those which have gone before and modifies in some way the quality of those which come after." John Dewey, *Experience and Education* (New York: Free Press, 1997), 35.

8. Constance Perin, *Shouldering Risks: The Culture of Control in the Nuclear Power Industry* (Princeton, NJ: Princeton University Press, 2006), xvi.

9. For a more detailed description of relationships, risk, and HROs, see Jerry Busby and Marian Iszatt-White, "The Relational Aspect to High

Reliability Organization," *Journal of Contingencies and Crisis Management* 22, no. 2 (2014): 69–80.

10. Roe and Schulman, *High Reliability Management*, 42.

11. Ibid., 138.

12. Dorwin Cartwright, "Lewinian Theory as a Contemporary Systematic Framework," in *Psychology: A Study of a Science*, ed. Sigmund Koch. (New York: McGraw-Hill, 1959), 7–91, see 10–21.

13. Kurt Lewin, *Principles of Topological Psychology* (New York: McGraw-Hill, 1936), 34–36.

14. Diane Vaughan, "The Dark Side of Organizations: Mistakes, Misconduct, and Disaster," *Annual Review of Sociology* 25 (1999): 271–305, see 280–281.

15. This sign now hangs over the desk of the Karl Weick.

16. Dill, "Staying Alive."

17. The three states of mind are summarized from Don Reid, *Rock Climbing: Yosemite Free Climbs* (Helena, MT: Falcon Press, 1998), 8–21.

18. John Dewey, *Experience and Nature* (New York: Dover, 1925/1958), 158. Note the similarity of existing events + foreseen events to the earlier discussion of "mental contrasting."

19. Ann Langley and Hari Tsoukas, "Introducing 'Perspectives on Process Organization Studies,'" in *Process, Sensemaking, and Organizing*, Perspectives on Process Organization Studies ed. Tor Hernes and Sally Maitlis (Oxford, United Kingdom: Oxford University Press, 2010), 1–26.

20. FOD walk downs were described earlier in Chapter 3 under the heading "The Mind-Set for Preoccupation with Failure."

21. Karlene H. Roberts and Denise M. Rousseau, "Research in Nearly Failure-Free, High-Reliability Organizations Having the Bubble," *IEEE Transactions on Engineering Management* 36 (1989): 132–139.

22. Gene I. Rochlin, *Trapped in the Net: The Unanticipated Consequences of Computerization* (Princeton: Princeton University Press, 1997), 109, italics added.

23. Mica R. Endsley, "The Role of Situation Awareness in Naturalistic Decision Making," in *Naturalistic Decision Making*, Expertise: Research and Applications, ed. Caroline E. Zsambok and Gary Klein (Mahwah, NJ: Erlbaum, 1997), 270.

24. Sidney Dekker, *Drift into Failure* (Burlington, VT: Ashgate, 2011).

25. Todd R. LaPorte, "The United States Air Traffic System: Increasing Reliability in the Midst of Rapid Growth," in *The Development of Large Technical Systems*, ed. Renate Mayntz and Thomas P. Hughes. (Boulder, CO: Westview Press, 1988), 215–244, see 224.

26. Emile M. Roth, "Analysis of Decision Making in Nuclear Power Plant Emergencies: An Investigation of Aided Decision Making," in *Naturalistic*

Decision Making, Expertise: Research and Applications ed. Caroline E. Zsambok and Gary Klein (Mahwah, NJ: Erlbaum, 1997), 175–182.

27. Roth, "Analysis of Decision Making," 180.

28. Roth, "Analysis of Decision Making," 181.

29. Roth, "Analysis of Decision Making," 179.

30. See similar interaction patterns in railroad operations in Emilie M. Roth, Jordan Multer, and Thomas Raslear, "Shared Situation Awareness as a Contributor to High Reliability Performance in Railroad Operations," *Organization Studies* 27, no. 7 (2006): 967–987.

31. Roth, "Analysis of Decision Making," 180.

32. Karl E. Weick and Karlene H. Roberts, "Collective Mind in Organizations: Heedful Interrelating on Flight Decks," *Administrative Science Quarterly* 38, no. 3 (1993): 357–381, quote on 357.

33. Jeremy S. Busby, "Failure to Mobilize in Reliability-Seeking Organizations: Two Cases from the UK Railways," *Journal of Management Studies* 43, no. 6 (2006): 1375–1393.

34. Busby, "Failure to Mobilize in Reliability-Seeking Organizations," 1390.

35. This analysis is adapted from Kathleen M. Sutcliffe and Karl E. Weick, "Information Overload Revisited," in *The Oxford Handbook of Organizational Decision Making*, ed. Gerard P. Hodgkinson and William H. Starbuck. (New York: Oxford University Press, 2008), 56–75.

36. The U.S. National Central Bureau (USNCB) for INTERPOL (international police organization) is an office under the control and direction of the Departments of Justice and Homeland Security. The U.S. authority for INTERPOL functions rests by law with the U.S. Attorney General. The USNCB serves as a point of contact for both American and foreign police seeking assistance in criminal investigations that extend beyond their national boundaries. Known within the international community as INTERPOL Washington, the USNCB brings together U.S. police at all levels, providing a neutral territory where jurisdictions and mandates are interwoven to permit cooperation and assistance to the fullest extent possible.

37. Robert B. Stacey, "Report on the Erroneous Fingerprint Individualization in the Madrid Train Bombing Case," *Forensic Science Communication* 7, no. 1 (2005): 1–12, see 11.

38. Robert B. Stacey, "A Report on the Erroneous Fingerprint Individualization in the Madrid Train Bombing Case," *Journal of Forensic Identification* 54, no. 6 (2004): 706–718.

39. Stacey, "A Report on the Erroneous Fingerprint Individualization," 2004, 711.

40. Ibid., 713.

41. Stacey, personal communication, 2005.

42. Stacey, "A Report on the Erroneous Fingerprint Individualization," 2004, 714–716.

43. For an example of just such a regression, see Karl E. Weick, "The Vulnerable System: An Analysis of the Tenerife Air Disaster," *Journal of Management* 16, no. 3 (1990): 571–593.

44. Stacey, "Report on the Erroneous Fingerprint Individualization," 2005, 10. This observation is relevant to Chapter 7, where we discuss deference to expertise.

45. Stacey, "Report on the Erroneous Fingerprint Individualization," 2005, 8, 11.

46. The phrase is found in Taylor and Van Every, *The Emergent Organization*, x: "The crucible of the quotidian is the ultimately determining factor in what the organization will be like. It is this that we mean by communication as the site of organization." If we take the phrase apart, then the word *crucible* = test, trial, melting of several, and the word *quotidian* = daily, commonplace, recurs every day.

47. Barton and Sutcliffe, "Overcoming Dysfunctional Momentum," 1331.

48. Ibid.

49. In saying this we do not ignore the disruption that interruptions can create. This disruption is evident, for example, when health-care personnel are preparing medications and are interrupted while doing so. To cut down on the resulting medication errors, hospitals have begun to create a "No Interruption Zone" that is physically marked off. See Kyle Anthony, C. Wiencek, C. Bauer, B. Daly, and M. K. Anthony, "No Interruptions Please: Impact of a No Interruption Zone on Medication Safety in Intensive Care Units," *Critical Care Nurse* 30, no. 3 (2010): 21–29.

50. A good example of the effects of slowing down to entertain a possible redirection of activity is found in Carol-Anne Moulton, G. Regehr, L. Lingard, C. Merritt, and H. MacRae, "Slowing Down to Stay Out of Trouble in the Operating Room: Remaining Attentive in Automaticity," *Academic Medicine* 85, no. 10 (2010): 1571–1577.

51. Dewey, *Human Nature and Conduct*, 127–128.

52. Rudolph, Morrison, and Carroll, "The Dynamics of Action-Oriented Problem Solving," 735.

53. John Dewey, "How, What, and What for in Social Inquiry," in *John Dewey: Later Works*, vol. 16, *1949–1952*, ed. Jo Ann Boydston (Carbondale, IL: Southern Illinois University Press, 2008), 333–340.

54. Barton and Sutcliffe, "Overcoming Dysfunctional Momentum," 1344.

55. See Barton and Sutcliffe, "Overcoming Dysfunctional Momentum," for more information about dysfunctional momentum.

56. The nominal group technique is a process that enables a group to generate a list of issues, problems, or solutions and to come to some agreement on the relative importance of these issues. The process allows for equal participation by all members of a group and puts quiet team members on equal footing with more dominant members. The process consists of a number of steps but goes something like this. First, generate a list of issues, problems, and solutions—have people write out their statements (or verbalize them if people feel safe bringing up controversial issues). Write the statements on a flip chart or board, and eliminate duplicates or clarify the meaning of the statements. Next, record the final list of statements on a flip chart or board, and assign them a number or letter. The next step is for each group member to record the corresponding letters for each statement and rank order them. Finally, combine the rankings of all the group members. The higher the resulting number for a statement, the higher its ranking (priority).

Chapter 6

1. Chris C. Demchak, "Lessons from the Military: Surprise, Resilience, and the Atrium Model," in *Designing Resilience: Preparing for Extreme Events*, ed. Louise K. Comfort, Arjen Boin, and Chris C. Demchak. (Pittsburgh, PA: University of Pittsburgh Press, 2010), 62–83, see 70.

2. Adapted from Aaron Wildavsky, *Searching for Safety*, Studies in Social Philosophy and Policy (New Brunswick, NJ: Transaction, 1991), 70.

3. See discussion of "failure to rescue" in Kathleen M. Sutcliffe and Karl E. Weick, "Mindful Organizing and Resilient Health Care," in *Resilient Health Care*, Resilient Health Care, ed. Erik Hollnagel, Jeffrey Braithwaite, and Robert L. Wears. (Farnham, Surrey, United Kingdom: Ashgate, 2013), 145–158.

4. Scott D. Sagan, *The Limits of Safety: Organizations, Accidents, and Nuclear Weapons* (Princeton, NJ: Princeton University Press, 1993), 241–242.

5. Paul Gleason, "LCES—A Key to Safety in the Wildland Fire Environment," *Fire Management Notes* 51, no. 4 (1991): 9.

6. Graham Danton, *The Theory and Practice of Seamanship*, 11th ed. (London: Routledge, 1996).

7. Arnold Barnett and Alexander Wang, "Passenger-Mortality Risk Estimates Provide Perspectives About Airline Safety," *Flight Safety Digest* 19, no. 4 (2000): 1–12, quoted in Sidney Dekker, *Safety Differently: Human Factors for a New Era*, 2nd ed. (Boca Raton, FL: CRC Press, 2015), 263.

8. Ted Putnam, personal communication to Karl Weick regarding the Dude Fire, 2003.

9. Brad Allenby and Jonathan Fink, "Toward Inherently Secure and Resilient Societies," *Science* 309, no. 5737 (August 2005): 1034–1036, see 1034.

10. Brian Walker and David Salt, *Resilience Thinking: Sustaining Ecosystems and People in a Changing World* (Washington, DC: Island Press, 2006), 164.

11. Erik Hollnagel, "The Four Cornerstones of Resilience Engineering," in *Resilience Engineering Perspectives*, vol. 2, *Preparation and Restoration*, ed. Christopher P. Nemeth, Erik Hollnagel, and Sidney Dekker (Farnham, Surrey, United Kingdom: Ashgate, 2009), 117–133, see 117.

12. Kathleen M. Sutcliffe and Timothy Vogus, "Organizing for Resilience," in *Positive Organizational Scholarship: Foundations of a New Discipline*, ed. Kim S. Cameron, Jane E. Dutton, and Robert E. Quinn (San Francisco: Berrett-Koehler, 2003), 94–110.

13. Robin Henig, *A Dancing Matrix: How Science Confronts Emerging Viruses* (New York: Vintage, 1993), 193–194, italics added.

14. Quoted in Henig, *A Dancing Matrix*, 193–194.

15. Eric B. Dent and Susan G. Goldberg, "Challenging 'Resistance to Change,'" *Journal of Applied Behavioral Science* 35, no. 1 (1999): 25–41.

16. Dent and Goldberg, "Challenging 'Resistance to Change,'" 25–41.

17. Recall the earlier discussion of improvisation as depicted by Gilbert Ryle that was included in our discussion of sense-discrediting in Chapter 4.

18. Donald A. Schön, *Educating the Reflective Practitioner: Toward a New Design for Teaching and Learning in the Professions* (San Francisco, CA: Jossey-Bass, 1987): 26–27.

19. Karl E. Weick, "Organizational Redesign as Improvisation," in *Organizational Change and Redesign: Ideas and Insights for Improving Performance*, ed. George P. Huber and William H. Glick. (New York: Oxford University Press, 1993): 346–379.

20. Westrum, "Thinking by Groups," 340.

21. Lucian L. Leape D. J. Cullen, M. D. Clapp, et al., "Pharmacists' Participation on Physician Rounds and Adverse Drug Events in the Intensive Care Unit," *Journal of the American Medical Association* 282, no. 3 (1999): 267–70.

22. Wildavsky, *Searching for Safety*, 120.

23. Joseph Trombello, *Miracle in the Cornfield* (Appleton, WI: Printsource Plus, 1999), 128.

24. Trombello, *Miracle in the Cornfield*, 133.

25. Laurence Gonzales, *Flight 232: A Story of Disaster and Survival* (New York: W. W. Norton, 2014), 50–51.

26. Trombello, *Miracle in the Cornfield*, 135.

27. A check airman is a person qualified to conduct flight checks of crew performance both in flight and in simulators.

28. Al Haynes, "The Crash of United Flight 232," speech delivered at NASA Ames Research Center, May 24, 1991, accessed January 2015, http://yarchive.net/air/airliners/dc10_sioux_city.html.

29. Haynes, "The Crash of United Flight 232."

30. The video can be accessed at http://youtu.be/Ovg5xTavEGY.

31. Haynes, "The Crash of United Flight 232."

32. Macarthur Job, *Air Disaster*, (Weston Creek, Australia: Aerospace Publications, 1996), 2: 195.

33. Claude Gilbert, "Planning for Catastrophe: How France Prepares for the Avian Flu and What It Means for Resilience," in *Designing Resilience: Preparing for Extreme Events*, ed. Louise K. Comfort, Arjen Boin, and Chris C. Demchak (Pittsburgh, PA: University of Pittsburgh Press, 2010), 180–195, see 195.

34. Haynes, "The Crash of United Flight 232."

35. Royal Aeronautical Society, "Crew Resource Management: A Paper by the CRM Standing Group of the Royal Aeronautical Society" (London, October 1999).

36. Tony Kern, *Redefining Airmanship* (New York: McGraw-Hill, 1997), 137.

37. Haynes, "The Crash of United Flight 232."

38. This is an excellent example of heedful interrelating (see earlier discussion in Chapter 5).

39. Haynes, "The Crash of United Flight 232."

40. Kern, *Redefining Airmanship*, 138.

41. Haynes, "The Crash of United Flight 232."

42. Demchak, "Lessons from the Military," 67.

43. Trombello, *Miracle in the Cornfield*, 129.

44. Weick, *The Social Psychology of Organizing*, 1st ed., 40.

45. Gabriel, *Organizing Words*, 212.

46. Haynes, "The Crash of United Flight 232."

47. Gilbert, "Planning for Catastrophe," 192–193.

48. Haynes, "The Crash of United Flight 232."

49. Ibid.

50. Trombello, *Miracle in the Cornfield*, 129.

51. Haynes, "The Crash of United Flight 232."

52. *Webster's New Dictionary of Synonyms*, s.v. "problematic" (Springfield, MA: Merriam-Webster, 1984).

53. Emery Roe, *Making the Most of Mess: Reliability and Policy in Today's Management Challenges* (Durham, NC: Duke University Press, 2013), 135.

54. See John F. Krafcik, "Triumph of the Lean Production System," *Sloan Management Review* 30, no. 1 (1988): 41–52. For a historical perspective on

lean production, see Matthias Holweg, "The Genealogy of Lean Production," *Journal of Operations Management* 25, no. 2 (2007): 420–437.

Chapter 7

1. Neil M. Agnew, Kenneth M. Ford, and Patrick J. Hayes, "Expertise in Context: Personally Constructed, Socially Selected and Reality-Relevant?" in *Expertise in Context: Human and Machine*, ed. Paul J. Feltovich, Kenneth M. Ford, and Robert R. Hoffman (Menlo Park, CA: AAAI Press, 1997), 219–244, quoted in Harald A. Mieg, *The Social Psychology of Expertise: Case Studies in Research, Professional Domains, and Expert Roles* (Mahwah, NJ: Erlbaum, 2001), 8.

2. Fred W. Frailey, "Union Pacific Traffic Jam," *Trains* (January 1998).

3. Columbia Accident Investigation Board, *Columbia Accident Investigation Board*, 201.

4. Ibid., 203, italics added.

5. Attributed to Alan Brunacini.

6. Lord Justice Taylor, *Hillsborough Stadium Disaster: Interim Report* (London: Her Majesty's Stationery Office, April 15, 1989), accessed January 2015 at http://www.southyorks.police.uk/sites/default/files/Taylor%20Interim%20Report.pdf, 49.

7. John N. Maclean, *Fire on the Mountain: The True Story of the South Canyon Fire* (New York: William Morrow, 1999).

8. Rochlin, "Informal Organizational Networking," 159–176.

9. Roberts, Stout, and Halpern, "Decision Dynamics," 614–624.

10. Weick, Sutcliffe, and Obstfeld, "Organizing for High Reliability," 102.

11. Karl E. Weick and Kathleen M. Sutcliffe, *Managing the Unexpected: Assuring High Performance in an Age of Complexity* (San Francisco, CA: Jossey-Bass, 2001).

12. Rochlin, "Informal Organizational Networking."

13. Roberts, Stout, and Halpern, "Decision Dynamics," 622.

14. Weick, Sutcliffe, and Obstfeld, "Organizing for High Reliability."

15. Michael D. Cohen, Roger Burkhart, Giovanni Dosi, Massimo Egidi, Luigi Marengo, Massimo Warglien and Sidney Winter, "Routines and Other Recurring Action Patterns of Organizations: Contemporary Research Issues," *Industrial and Corporate Change* 5, no. 3 (1996): 653–698.

16. Dekker, *Safety Differently*, 261.

17. Harald Mieg, "Social and Sociological Factors in the Development of Expertise," in *The Cambridge Handbook of Expertise and Expert Performance*,

Cambridge Handbooks in Psychology, ed. K. Anders Ericsson, Neil Charness, Paul J. Feltovich, and Robert R. Hoffman. (New York: Cambridge University Press, 2006), 743–760, see 746.

18. Harald A. Mieg, *The Social Psychology of Expertise: Case Studies in Research, Professional Domains, and Expert Roles*, Expertise: Research and Applications, (Mahwah, NJ: Erlbaum, 2001), 45.

19. Michael Bacon, *Pragmatism* (Malden, MA: Polity, 2012), 54.

20. Dorothy Leonard-Barton and Walter C. Swap, *Deep Smarts: How to Cultivate and Transfer Enduring Business Wisdom* (Cambridge, MA: Harvard Business Press, 2005), 57.

21. Leonard-Barton and Swap, *Deep Smarts*, 47.

22. Anna T. Canciolo, C. Matthew, R. J. Sternberg, and R.K. Wagner, "Tacit Knowledge, Practical Intelligence, and Expertise," in *The Cambridge Handbook of Expertise and Expert Performance*, Cambridge Handbooks in Psychology, ed. K. Anders Ericsson, Neil Charness, Paul J. Feltovich, and Robert R. Hoffman. (New York: Cambridge University Press, 2006), 613–632, see 614–615.

23. Paul J. Feltovich, Michael Prietula, and K. Anders Ericsson, "Studies of Expertise from Psychological Perspectives," in *The Cambridge Handbook of Expertise and Expert Performance*, Cambridge Handbooks in Psychology, eds. K. Anders Ericsson, Neil Charness, Paul J. Feltovich, and Robert R. Hoffman. (New York: Cambridge University Press, 2006), 41–68, see 47, italics added.

24. Mieg, *The Social Psychology of Expertise*, 43.

25. John Dewey, *Psychology* (New York: Harper and Brothers, 1886), 142.

26. Leonard-Barton and Swap, *Deep Smarts*, 41.

27. Kathleen M. Sutcliffe and Timothy Vogus, "Organizing for Resilience," in *Positive Organizational Scholarship* eds. Kim S. Cameron, Jane E. Dutton, and Robert E. Quinn (San Francisco: Berrett-Koehler, 2003), 94–110, italics added.

28. Jordan M. Scher, ed., *Theories of the Mind* (New York: Free Press, 1962).

29. Cynthia Renaud, "The Missing Piece of NIMS: Teaching Incident Commanders How to Function in the Edge of Chaos," *Homeland Security Affairs* 8 (June 2012): 2–18.

30. Barton and Sutcliffe, "Overcoming Dysfunctional Momentum."

31. Barton and Sutcliffe, "Overcoming Dysfunctional Momentum," 1341, italics in original.

32. Ibid.

33. Roberts, Stout, and Halpern, "Decision Dynamics," 622.

34. Ibid.

35. David D. Woods, Emily S. Patterson, and Emile M. Roth, "Can We Ever Escape From Data Overload? A Cognitive Systems Diagnosis," *Cognition, Technology & Work* 4 (2002): 22–36, see 27.

36. Michelle Barton, Kathleen Sutcliffe, Timothy Vogus, and Theodore DeWitt, "Performing under Uncertainty: Contextualized Engagement in Wildland Firefighting," *Journal of Contingencies and Crisis Management* 23, no. 2 (2015): 74–83.

37. Paul R. Schulman, Emery Roe, Michael van Eeten, Mark de Bruijne, "High Reliability and the Management of Critical Infrastructures," *Journal of Contingencies and Crisis Management* 12, no. 1 (2004): 14–28; Roe, *Making the Most of Mess*.

38. Notice how well this describes the actions of the crew in the UA 232 incident discussed earlier in Chapter 6 as an example of resilient acting. Roe and Schulman, *High Reliability Management*, 24.

39. The preceding fourfold distinction is elaborated in Roe and Schulman, *High Reliability Management*, chap. 3, 41–49.

40. Schulman et al., "High Reliability and the Management of Critical Infrastructures," 16.

41. Mieg, "Social and Sociological Factors in the Development of Expertise," 751.

42. Leonard-Barton and Swap, *Deep Smarts*, 12.

43. See the earlier comment on situated humility in the discussion of sensitivity to operations.

44. Barton and Sutcliffe, "Overcoming Dysfunctional Momentum," 1344.

45. For a more in-depth treatment of hubris, see Pasquale M. Picone, Giovanni B. Dagnino, and Anna Minà, "The Origin of Failure: A Multidisciplinary Appraisal of the Hubris Hypothesis and Proposed Research Agenda," *The Academy of Management Perspectives* 28, no. 4 (2014): 447–468.

46. Columbia Accident Investigation Board, *Columbia Accident Investigation Board*, 344.

47. Gary Klein, "Performing a Project Premortem," *Harvard Business Review* 85, no. 9 (2007): 18–19.

48. Westrum, "Thinking by Groups."

49. Michelle A. Barton and Kathleen M. Sutcliffe, "Learning When to Stop Momentum," *Sloan Management Review* (April 2010): 71.

Chapter 8

1. Lou Gerstner Jr., *Who Says Elephants Can't Dance?* (New York: Harper, 2002), 180–181.

2. Gerstner Jr., *Who Says Elephants Can't Dance?*, 185–186.

3. Gabriel, *Organizing Words*, 65.

4. Barry A. Turner and Nick F. Pidgeon, *Man-Made Disasters*, 2nd ed. (Oxford, United Kingdom: Butterworth-Heinemann, 1997), 47.

5. *American Heritage Dictionary*, s.v. "imbue," 2nd ed. (New York: Houghton-Mifflin, 1982).

6. Chris Argyris, "Some Problems in Conceptualizing Organizational Climate: A Case Study of a Bank," *Administrative Science Quarterly* 2, no. 4 (1958): 501–520.

7. Eric M. Eisenberg, "Jamming Transcendence through Organizing," *Communication Research*, 17, no. 2 (1990): 139–164.

8. Alfred Schutz, "The Stranger," in *Collected Papers*, vol. 2, *Studies in Social Theory*, ed. Arvid Brodersen (The Hague, Netherlands: Martinus Nijhoff, 1964), 91–105.

9. Barry A. Turner, "The Organizational and Interorganizational Development of Disasters," *Administrative Science Quarterly* 21 (1976): 378–397.

10. See Stian Antonsen, *Safety Culture: Theory, Method and Improvement* (Burlington, VT: Ashgate, 2009), 27–41 for a detailed analysis of Meyerson and Martin. Also see Anne Richter and Christian Koch, "Integration, Differentiation and Ambiguity in Safety Cultures," *Safety Science* 42 (2004): 703–722.

11. Debra Meyerson and Joanne Martin, "Cultural Change: An Integration of Three Different Views," *Journal of Management Studies* 24, no. 6 (1987): 623–647, see p. 637.

12. Tony J. Watson, *In Search of Management: Culture, Chaos and Control in Managerial Work* (London: South-Western/Cengage, 2001), 21.

13. Gabriel, *Organizing Words*, 312.

14. For a more detailed discussion of these contributions, see Ian D. Colville, Robert H. Waterman, and Karl E. Weick, "Organizing and the Search for Excellence: Making Sense of the Times in Theory and Practice," *Organization* 6, no. 1 (1999): 129–148.

15. Thomas J. Peters and Robert H. Waterman Jr., *In Search of Excellence: Lessons from America's Best-Run Companies* (New York: Harper and Row, 1982). The relevant contribution regarding culture is in Chapter 12, "Simultaneous Loose-Tight Properties." On p. 322, Peters and Waterman put the point about simultaneity this way: "Autonomy is a product of discipline. The discipline ([instilled by] a few shared values) provides the framework. It gives people confidence (to experiment for instance) stemming from stable expectations about what really counts. . . . The discipline of a small number of shared values induces practical autonomy and experimentation throughout the organization." A culture with three or four key values that have been converted into norms for appropriate behavior is more likely to be coordinated and resilient.

16. Ahmet Atak and Sytze Kingma, "Safety Culture in an Aircraft Maintenance Organization: A View from the Inside," *Safety Science* 49 (2011): 268–278.

17. Karl E. Weick, "Organizational Culture as a Source of High Reliability," *California Management Review* 29 (1987): 124.

18. Edgar H. Schein, *Organizational Culture and Leadership* (San Francisco: Jossey-Bass, 1985), 7–22. Definition is adapted from Chapter 1.

19. Gabriel, *Organizing Words*, 66.

20. This close blending of culture with expectations has been noted by other researchers of culture, such as Charles O'Reilly III, "Corporations, Culture, and Commitment: Motivation and Social Control in Organizations," *California Management Review* 31 (1989): 9–25.

21. Antonsen, *Safety Culture*, 4.

22. O'Reilly III, "Corporations, Culture, and Commitment" 9–25.

23. See James P. Womack, Daniel T. Jones, and Daniel Roos, *The Machine that Changed the World* (London: Simon & Schuster, 1990). Also see Jeffrey Liker, *The Toyota Way: 14 Management Principles from the World's Greatest Manufacturer* (New York: McGraw-Hill, 2004). In 2007 (fiscal year 2008) Toyota earned $19.9 billion. It was the fiftieth consecutive year of profits for the company.

24. Michael A. Cusamano, "Technology Strategy and Management: Reflections on the Toyota Debacle," *Communications of the ACM* 54, no. 1 (January 2011): 34.

25. Although we develop a chronological treatment of variations in Toyota's performance, readers may also want to examine a comparison between the more traditional Toyota and the less traditional Hyundai, reported in Richard M. Steers and Won Shul Shim, "Strong Leaders, Strong Cultures: Global Management Lessons from Toyota and Hyundai," *Organizational Dynamics* 42, no. 3 (2013): 217–227.

26. See Asmita Joshi's description of the precursors to TPS. As Joshi notes in "Product Recalls: A Failure of Toyota Production System," *ASM's International E-Journal of Ongoing Research in Management and IT* (2013), accessed July 14, 2014, http://www.asmgroup.edu.in/incon/publication/incon13-gen-048.pdf, 3, Toyota received its inspiration for the TPS not from the American auto industry but from visiting a supermarket. A delegation from Toyota led by a Toyota engineer, Taiicho Ohno, first visited several Ford Motor plants in Michigan and were "unimpressed and even appalled" by ineffective methods, high levels of inventory, uneven processes, and large amounts of daily rework. A subsequent visit to a supermarket where the delegation observed how the supermarket reordered and restocked goods only once customers had bought them proved inspirational. As Joshi points out: "Toyota applied the lesson from the

supermarket by reducing the amount of inventory they would hold only to a level that its employees would need for a small period of time, and then subsequently reorder. This would become the precursor of the now-famous Just in Time (JIT) inventory system" (p. 3). Also see Toyota Motor Corporation, "Toyota Traditions," March 2004, accessed May 31, 2014, http://www.toyota-global.com/company/toyota_traditions/quality/mar_apr_2004.html.

27. Joshi, *Product Recalls*, 3.

28. Anthony P. Andrews, John Simon, Feng Tian, and Jun Zhao, "The Toyota Crisis: An Economic Operational and Strategic Analysis of the Massive Recall," *Management Research Review* 34, no. 10 (2011): 1067.

29. Liker, *The Toyota Way*, 35–42. The 14 principles constituting the Toyota Way can be organized into four broad categories: (1) Long-term philosophy at the expense of short-term financial goals, (2) The right process will produce the right results, (3) Add value to the organization by developing your people, and (4) Continuously solving root problems drives organizational learning. The first principle involves managing with a long view rather than for short-term gain. It reflects a belief that people need purpose to find motivation and establish goals. The next seven principles relate to work processes, with an eye toward reliability and quality as outcomes. The principles in this section deal with work process redesign to eliminate waste and empowering employees in the face of Toyota's bureaucratic processes to ensure the process of continuous improvement (*kaizen*). Any employee has the authority to stop production to signal a quality issue, emphasizing that quality takes precedence. These seven principles include creating continuous process flows to bring problems to the surface, using pull systems to avoid overproduction, leveling out workloads (work like the tortoise, not the hare), building a culture of stopping to fix problems to get quality right the first time, standardizing tasks and processes as a means to empower employees and improve continuously, using visual controls to make problems transparent, and using only reliable, thoroughly tested technology. Principles 9 through 11 concern human development. Principle nine emphasizes the need to ensure that leaders embrace and promote the corporate philosophy. This reflects, according to Liker, a belief that the principles have to be ingrained in employees to survive. The tenth principle emphasizes the need of individuals and work teams to embrace the company's philosophy, with teams of four to five people who are judged in success by their team achievements, rather than their individual efforts. Principle 11 proposes respect for network partners and suppliers and concern with challenging them and helping them improve. The final three principles embrace a philosophy of problem solving that emphasizes thorough understanding of problems (going to see for oneself), consensus-based decision making, and

relentless reflection and continuous improvement. According to Liker, the process of becoming a learning organization involves criticizing every aspect of what one does.

30. Recall the earlier discussion of loose-tight connections around values and the Peters and Waterman Jr. observation that, in the interest of flexibility and order, tight coupling should occur around no more than three or four values. If we treat Peters and Waterman Jr. as prescriptive, then Toyota had 79 percent more values than would allow for a combination of centralization and decentralization.

31. Liker, *The Toyota Way*, 36.

32. Toyota Motor Corporation, *Environmental and Social Report 2004* (Toyota Motor Corporation: July 2004), accessed July 14, 2014, http://www.toyota-global.com/sustainability/report/sr/04/pdf/e_s_report_2004.pdf, 64.

33. Toyota, *Environmental and Social Report 2004*, 64. Also see Liker, *The Toyota Way*, xi: Foreword by Gary Convis, managing officer of Toyota and president of Toyota Motor Manufacturing, Kentucky.

34. Liker, *The Toyota Way*, 24.

35. Toyota, *Environmental and Social Report 2004*, 64.

36. Ibid.

37. Ibid.

38. Jeffrey K. Liker and Timothy N. Ogden, *Toyota Under Fire: Lessons for Turning Crisis into Opportunity* (New York: McGraw-Hill, 2012).

39. Alexandra Frean, "Fears Over Potential Toyota Problems Surfaced in 2006, U.S. Senate Told," *Times Online*, March 3, 2010, accessed June 8, 2015, http://www.thetimes.co.uk/tto/business/industries/engineering/article2462194.ece.

40. Robert E. Cole, "What Really Happened to Toyota," *MIT Sloan Management Review* 52, no. 4 (2011): 29–36.

41. Rebecca J. Meisenbach and Sarah B. Feldner, "Toyota—Oh, What a Feeling, or Oh, What a Mess?: Ethics at the Intersection of Industry, Government, and Publics," in *Case Studies in Organizational Communication: Ethical Perspectives and Practices*, ed. Steve May (Los Angeles: Sage, 2013), 111–124. See also Bill Vlasic, "Toyota's Slow Awakening to a Deadly Problem," *New York Times*, January 31, 2010, 1A.

42. Vlasic, "Toyota's Slow Awakening," 1A.

43. Meisenbach and Feldner, "Toyota—Oh, What a Feeling," 99–100.

44. Meisenbach and Feldner, "Toyota—Oh, What a Feeling," 100.

45. Cusamano, "Technology Strategy and Management," 34.

46. Cusamano, "Technology Strategy and Management," 33; Cole, "What Really Happened to Toyota."

47. Cusamano, "Technology Strategy and Management," 33.

48. Cole, "What Really Happened to Toyota."

49. The Union of Japanese Scientists and Engineers received a request by Toyota in March 2010. The panel consisted of four people: two professors and experts in quality control, a prominent automotive journalist, and a consumer spokesperson. It released its report, titled *Findings by Independent Experts about Quality Assurance at Toyota*, on June 30, 2010 (see http://www.toyota-prospekte.de/index.php?page=Attachment&attachmentID=130&h=6456e6e8b3dcd17f5ea97dadb182f22e0869c3e9, accessed July 15, 2014). The North American Quality Advisory Panel (NAQAP) was announced on April 29, 2010. It consisted of seven members, including a past U.S. secretary of transportation (Rodney Slater), two prominent corporate leaders, a former member of the National Transportation Safety Board, and three prominent professors with varied other expertise. It released its interim report, titled *A Road Forward: The Report of the Toyota North American Quality Advisory Panel*, in May 2011 (see http://www.changinggears.info/wp-content/uploads/2011/05/EMBARGOED_COPY_Toyota_Quality_Advisory_Panel_Report.pdf, accessed July 15, 2014).

50. NAQAP, *A Road Forward*, 3–4. See also the Union of Japanese Scientists and Engineers, *Findings by Independent Experts*.

51. NAQAP, *A Road Forward*, 4.

52. *Guardian*, "Toyota President Akio Toyoda's Statement to Congress," *Guardian*, February 24, 2010, accessed March 14, 2014, http://www.theguardian.com/business/2010/feb/24/akio-toyoda-statement-to-congress/print.

53. Ibid. Also see Meisenbach and Feldner, "Toyota—Oh, What a Feeling," 101–104; Andrews et al., "The Toyota Crisis."

54. Takahiro Fujimoto, "Under the Hood of Toyota's Recall: 'A Tremendous Expansion of Complexity,'" interview by John Paul MacDuffie, *Knowledge@Wharton*, March 31, 2010, accessed July 15, 2014, http://knowledge.wharton.upenn.edu/article.cfm?articleid=2462.

55. NAQAP, *A Road Forward*, 28.

56. NAQAP, *A Road Forward*, 29.

57. *Response by Toyota and NHTSA to Incidents of Sudden Unintended Acceleration: Hearing Before the Subcomm. on Oversight and Investigations of the H. Comm. on Energy and Commerce*, 111th Cong. 140 (2010) (statement of James E. Lentz, President and Chief Executive Officer of TMS), quoted in NAQAP, *A Road Forward*, 28.

58. Union of Japanese Scientists and Engineers, *Findings by Independent Experts*, 17–18.

59. NAQAP, *A Road Forward*, 3.

60. NAQAP, *A Road Forward*, 8; Union of Japanese Scientists and Engineers, *Findings by Independent Experts*, 6, 9.

61. NAQAP, *A Road Forward*, 24.

62. Ibid., 23. Similarly, before the 2007 Camry launch in the United States, Japanese consumers had complained about a "knocking" problem in their cars. Although Toyota fixed the Camry "knocking" problem in Japan as early as August 2006, U.S. consumers reported similar problems. It would appear that Toyota could have easily fixed the Camry problems in the United States, because the problems in America were similar to those in Japan. However, because Toyota was unable to recognize that these problems were one and the same, they took over a year for the company to resolve.

63. Akio Toyoda, "Toyota's Plan to Repair its Public Image," *Washington Post*, February 9, 2010, accessed May 31, 2014, http://www.washingtonpost.com/wp-dyn/content/article/2010/02/08/AR2010020803078.html.

64. NAQAP, *A Road Forward*, 23.

65. Ibid., 8.

66. Ibid.

67. CNN, "Toyota President Won't Attend U.S. Congress Hearing," *CNN*, February 17, 2010, accessed May 31, 2014, http://www.cnn.com/2010/BUSINESS/02/17/japan.toyota.press.conference/index.html.

68. Associated Press, "Toyota Probes Corolla Steering, Considers Recall," *WBUR*, February 17, 2010, accessed May 31, 2014, http://www.wbur.org/2010/02/17/toyota-corolla.

69. Justin McCurry, "Toyota Boss Agrees to Attend Congress hearing," *Guardian*, February 19, 2010, accessed May 31, 2014, http://www.guardian.co.uk/business/2010/feb/19/toyota-boss-congress-car-safety-recall; Mark Schone and Lisa Stark, "Toyota Boss Agrees to Come to Washington to Testify," *ABC News*, February 18, 2010, accessed May 31, 2014, http://abcnews.go.com/Blotter/RunawayToyotas/congress-asks-toyota-ceo-akio-toyoda-washington/story?id=9874584#.T7qDCOgV2qI.

70. NAQAP, *A Road Forward*, 8, 22, and 28; Union of Japanese Scientists and Engineers, *Findings by Independent Experts*, 8–9.

71. NAQAP, *A Road Forward*, 22.

72. Takahiro Fujimoto, "Under the Hood of Toyota's Recall."

73. NAQAP, *A Road Forward*, 25.

74. NAQAP, *A Road Forward*, 26, 39. The NAQAP suggested that Toyota go beyond this to create safety officers in each local market to deal with and report on local safety issues.

75. Ibid., 32.

76. Ibid.

Chapter 9

1. Richard I. Cook and David D. Woods, "Operating at the Sharp End," 304.

2. Paraphrased from Paul R. Schulman, "The Negotiated Order of Organizational Reliability."

3. Paraphrased from Karl E. Weick, Kathleen M. Sutcliffe, and David Obstfeld, "Organizing and the Process of Sensemaking," *Organization Science* 16, no. 4 (2005): 409–421.

4. Discussion of the Bhopal incident is based in part on analyses in Karl E. Weick, "Enacted Sensemaking in Crisis Situations," *Journal of Management Studies* 25, no. 4 (1988): 305–317, and Karl E. Weick, "Reflections on Enacted Sensemaking in the Bhopal Disaster," *Journal of Management Studies* 47, no. 3 (2010): 537–550. See also Edward Broughton, "The Bhopal Disaster and Its Aftermath: A Review," *Environmental Health* 4, no. 6 (2005), http://www.ehjournal.net/content/4/1/6.

5. Dominique Lapierre and Javier Moro, *Five Past Midnight in Bhopal* (New York: Warner, 2002), 291.

6. Lapierre and Moro, *Five Past Midnight*, 285.

7. Lapierre and Moro, *Five Past Midnight*, 292.

8. Erving Goffman, *Frame Analysis: An Essay on the Organization of Experience* (Cambridge, MA: Harvard University Press, 1974), 30.

9. Herbert Blumer, *Symbolic Interactionism: Perspective and Method* (Englewood Cliffs, NJ: Prentice-Hall, 1969), 168.

10. Robert Irwin, *Notes Toward a Model in Exhibition Catalog for the Robert Irwin Exhibition* (New York: Whitney Museum of American Art, April 16 to May 29, 1977), 25–26.

11. Barbara Czarniawska, *A Theory of Organizing*, 2nd ed. (Northampton, MA: Edward Elgar Publishing, 2014), 6.

12. Wendy K. Smith and Marianne W. Lewis, "Toward a Theory of Paradox: A Dynamic Equilibrium Model of Organizing," *Academy of Management Review* 36, no. 2 (2011): 381–403.

13. *Webster's New Dictionary of Synonyms*, s.v. "paradox" (Springfield, MA: Merriam-Webster, 1984).

14. *Webster's New Dictionary of Synonyms*, s.v. "anomaly" and "paradox" (Springfield, MA: Merriam-Webster, 1984), 592.

15. Ibid.

16. Gene I. Rochlin, "Defining 'High Reliability' Organizations in Practice: A Taxonomic Prologue," in *New Challenges to Understanding Organizations*, ed. Karlene Roberts. (New York: Macmillan, 1993), 11–32, see 24.

17. Todd R. LaPorte, "Complexity and Uncertainty: Challenge to Action," in *Organized Social Complexity*, ed. Todd R. LaPorte. (Princeton, NJ: Princeton University Press, 1975), 332–356, see 345.

18. Weick, *The Social Psychology of Organizing*, 2nd ed., 217–224.

19. Eric M. Eisenberg, Alexandra Murphy, Kathleen M. Sutcliffe, Robert Wears, Stephen Schenkel, Shawna Perry, and Mary Vanderhoef, "Communication in Emergency Medicine: Implications for Patient Safety," *Communication Monographs* 72, no. 4 (2005): 390–413.

20. Paget, *The Unity of Mistakes*, 143.

21. Hubert L. Dreyfus, *Being-In-The-World: A Commentary on Heidegger's Being and Time, Division I* (Boston, MA: MIT Press, 1991).

22. Gilbert, "Planning for Catastrophe," 192–193.

23. Rochlin, LaPorte, and Roberts, "The Self-Designing High Reliability Organization," 76–90.

24. Karl E. Weick, "Sensemaking in Organizations: Small Structures with Large Consequences," in *Social Psychology in Organizations: Advances in Theory and Research*, ed. Keith Murnighan (Englewood Cliffs, NJ: Prentice Hall, 1993), 10–37. Also see Karl E. Weick and Kathleen M. Sutcliffe, "Hospitals as Cultures of Entrapment: A Reanalysis of the Bristol Royal Infirmary," *California Management Review* 45, no. 2 (2003): 73–84; Carol Tavris and Elliot Aronson, *Mistakes Were Made (But Not by Me): Why We Justify Foolish Beliefs, Bad Decisions, and Hurtful Acts* (Boston: Houghton Mifflin Harcourt, 2008).

25. Weick and Sutcliffe, "Hospitals as Cultures of Entrapment." Also see Weick and Sutcliffe, *Managing the Unexpected*, 2nd ed., 109–138.

26. For the sake of balance it is important to acknowledge that there are times when escalating a commitment can prove beneficial. This possibility is explored thoughtfully in Helga Drummond, "Escalation of Commitment: When To Stay the Course?" *The Academy of Management Perspectives* 28, no. 4 (2014): 430–446.

27. William James, "Remarks on Spencer's Definition of Mind as Correspondence" *William James: Writings 1878–1899* (New York: Library of America, 1992), 908.

28. For more information about Paul Gleason, read Paul Gleason, "Leaders We Would Like to Meet—Paul Gleason," interview by Jim Cook and Angela Tom, accessed January 2015, http://www.fireleadership.gov/toolbox/leaders_meet/interviews/leaders_PaulGleason.html.

29. William James, *Some Problems of Philosophy* (Lincoln, NE: University of Nebraska Press, 1911/1996), 15.

30. Weick and Sutcliffe, *Managing the Unexpected*, 2nd ed.

31. Edgar H. Schein, *The Corporate Culture Survival Guide: Sense and Nonsense about Culture Change* (San Francisco: Jossey-Bass, 1999), 189. Also see Schein, *Organizational Culture and Leadership*, 299. For a more comprehensive discussion of Schein's views on system change in general, see Edgar H. Schein, "Models and Tools for Stability and Change in Human Systems," *Reflections* 4, no. 2 (2002): 34–46.

32. Jill Lepore, "The Disruption Machine: What the Gospel of Innovation Gets Wrong," *New Yorker*, June 23, 2014, http://www.newyorker.com/magazine/2014/06/23/the-disruption-machine.

33. Alan Deutschman, *Change or Die: The Three Keys to Change at Work and in Life* (New York: Harper, 2008).

34. Pat Lagadec, *Preventing Chaos in a Crisis: Strategies for Prevention, Control, and Damage Limitation* (London: McGraw-Hill International, 1993), 54.

35. Karl E. Weick, "Enacting an Environment: The Infrastructure of Organizing," in *Debating Organization: Point-Counterpoint in Organization Studies*, ed. Robert Westwood and Stewart Clegg (Malden, MA: Blackwell, 2003), 184–194, see 190.

About the Authors

Karl E. Weick

Karl E. Weick is the Rensis Likert Distinguished University Professor Emeritus of Organizational Behavior and Psychology at the University of Michigan. Weick joined the Stephen M. Ross School of Business at the University of Michigan in 1988 after previous faculty positions at the University of Texas, Cornell University, the University of Minnesota, and Purdue University. His PhD is from Ohio State University in Social and Organizational Psychology. He is a former editor of the journal *Administrative Science Quarterly* (1977–1985) and former associate editor of the journal *Organizational Behavior and Human Performance* (1971–1977).

Weick's book *The Social Psychology of Organizing*, first published in 1969 and revised in 1979, was designated one of the nine best business books ever written by *Inc.* magazine in December 1996. This work has also been profiled in *Wired* magazine and by Thomas J. Peters and Robert H. Waterman Jr. in their book, *In Search of Excellence*. The organizing formulation has more recently been expanded into a book titled *Sensemaking in Organizations* (Sage, 1995). Weick was presented with the Irwin Award for Distinguished Scholarly Contributions by the Academy of Management in 1990. In the same year he received the Best Article of the Year award from the *Academy of Management Review* for his article "Theory Construction as Disciplined Imagination."

Weick's research interests include collective sensemaking under pressure, handoffs and transitions in dynamic events, organizing for resilient performance, and continuous change.

Kathleen M. Sutcliffe

Kathleen M. Sutcliffe is a Bloomberg Distinguished Professor of Business and Medicine at Johns Hopkins University and the Gilbert and Ruth Whitaker Professor Emerita of Business Administration at the Stephen M. Ross School of Business at the University of Michigan. Sutcliffe joined Johns Hopkins University in 2014, after 20 years at the Ross School of Business. Prior to completing her PhD in management from the University of Texas at Austin in 1991, she lived and worked in Juneau, Alaska, as a program consultant for the state of Alaska and in Anchorage, Alaska, as a senior manager for the Aleutian Pribilof Islands Association, one of the regional Alaska Native health corporations.

In 2012 Sutcliffe was appointed by the National Academy of Sciences Institute of Medicine to a research panel to study workforce resilience in the Department of Homeland Security. In 2006 Sutcliffe received the Researcher of the Year award from the Ross School of Business for her research excellence.

Sutcliffe's research interests include topics such as organizational resilience and reliability, how organizations and their members sense emerging problems and cope with uncertainty, safety culture, and team and organizational learning. Her most recent work examines how elements of an organizational system influence errors in high-risk settings, such as wildland firefighting, oil and gas exploration, and health care. She has consulted with multinational corporations, government organizations, and nongovernmental organizations across the world.

Index